INTRODUCTION TO
Existentialism

By MARJORIE GRENE

THE UNIVERSITY OF CHICAGO PRESS

CHICAGO & LONDON

FIRST PUBLISHED UNDER THE TITLE

Dreadful Freedom

TO DAVID

THE UNIVERSITY OF CHICAGO PRESS, CHICAGO 60637
The University of Chicago Press, Ltd., London W. C. 1

FOREWORD

THIS is, in the main, an introductory essay; it is certainly in no sense an attempt at an exhaustive or definitive treatment of existentialism. There are numerous technical questions—such as Sartre's relation to phenomenology or psychoanalysis, for instance—which might well be dealt with at greater length; so might, in a different context, such problems as the existential treatment of time in its relation to other contemporary movements in philosophy and so on. It seemed wiser, however, for the reader's, as well as for the author's, sake to follow through a single, fairly simple theme: existentialism as the attempt at a new "revaluation of values" and its interpretation, in this light, of the individual in himself and in his relation to others.

Chapters ii and vi and parts of chapters iii and iv appeared as articles in the *Kenyon Review* in 1947. My thanks are due to the editors for their permission to reprint them, and to them, as well as to Professor Eliseo Vivas, of Ohio State University, and Professor Wallace Fowlie, of the University of Chicago, for their advice and encouragement. To my husband and to Mrs. Henri Frankfort I owe much more than I can say.

Acknowledgment is due the following publishers: to Librairie Gallimard, for permission to quote from *L'Être et le néant*; to Harcourt Brace and Company, for permission to quote from *The Republic of Silence*; to Fernand Aubier, for permission to quote from *Être et avoir*; to George Allen and Unwin, for permission to quote from Synge's *In Wicklow, West Kerry and Connemara*; to the editors of *Politics*, for permission to quote Mary McCarthy's translation of Simone de Beauvoir's *Eye for Eye*; to the editors of the *New Yorker*, for permission to quote Edmund Wilson's review of Sartre; and to M. Sartre, for permission to quote articles in *Les Temps modernes*.

PREFACE TO THE 1959 EDITION

IF I WERE writing this book now, I should correct it in three respects. First, it demands a chapter on the work of Paul Tillich. Especially in his recent publications, Tillich has shown how existentialism can issue in a living Christian philosophy. He has truly expressed the existential sense of dread and nothingness but has as truly transformed it in the light of worship. To add such a chapter would not alter my analysis of other authors, but it would put the existentialist tradition into a more just historical perspective. It would not be an addition, however, to make lightly, and I do not propose to make it now—only to confess that it ought to be there and that my "Postscript" would look rather different if it were.

Second, although I was concerned explicitly with existentialism as a "practical" philosophy, I could, I believe, have criticized it more adequately from more explicit theoretical premises. But I had no such premises at the time. If I were writing now on the same subject, I should start from the position developed in Michael Polanyi's *Personal Knowledge*. This is a theory of knowledge which, like Tillich's theology, both assimilates the truth of existentialism and successfully escapes its distressing narrowness. Again, to start from this point would be to put the achievements and the defects of existentialism in a truer light.

Finally, I had not, when I wrote this book, faced up to Heidegger's ontology. I could follow his argument on Being, I said then, only in the sense in which one might follow Alice down the rabbit hole. That was lazy. Since then I have tried

[v]

in earnest to find my way through this abominable wonder-land, and an ugly and almost empty wasteland it is. But since Heidegger has so loudly renounced existentialism and declared himself first and last a philosopher of Being, his "Quest for Being" ought to be reckoned with by his critics. Besides, if one is committed to an existentialist view of the nature of philosophical reflection, one has no right to take part of a man's philosophy out of its living context. Philosophy is "en situation" and does not come to bits—or if (as I believe to be the case with Heidegger) there are aspects of meaning in an otherwise meaningless whole, one should face the problem of the whole and recognize one's own distortion of the parts in one's extraction of them.

All these corrections would be by way of supplement; I would not unsay anything I said. But the first and second corrections admittedly would alter, I should hope for the better, my way of saying it.

MARJORIE GRENE

CLASH, RATHDRUM
CO. WICKLOW
IRELAND

TABLE OF CONTENTS

[vii]

CHAPTER ONE

WHY EXISTENTIALISM?

1

THE more fashionable a philosophy becomes, the more elusive is its definition. So the proponents of existentialism proclaim that, though many attack, few understand them. They insist on the essential optimism of their doctrine that "man makes himself," for there is always, until death, another chance. Granted, they would say, that, in their wide humanity, they explore the far corners of human life, the horrors and perversions uncharted by timorous captives of gentility. Granted, too, that, with honest ruthlessness, they expose the cant of a fraudulent, strictly bourgeois "human dignity." But just because of this very humaneness, this very honesty, they are decried as perverts and iconoclasts, as philosophic nihilists and artistic freaks. So, finally, as the word goes around, every treatise that dooms man to destruction, every novel whose characters are mad or bad, every play that depresses without elevating, is labeled "so existential"; and hence existentialism, more even than the naturalism of Zola or of Ibsen in their days, comes to mean the shocking, the sordid, or the obscene.

One may well agree with the existentialists that, so loosely used, the word is nearly meaningless—except perhaps for a vague sense that this movement, like others, expresses the collapse in our time of certain formerly cherished conventions—and that existentialists, in fiction as well as in philosophy, say a number of things that would undoubtedly have brought a blush to the cheek of the Podsnappian young person. But in that sense, after all, anyone, from Freud to

[1]

James Cain, might with more than justice be called an existentialist.

Nearly as meaningless, too, it seems to me, is the equally general, though much more serious, use of the word in some philosophic discussion, in which nearly every philosopher since Hegel is shown to be in some sense an existentialist. Again, there is truth in this usage, since existentialism is, in one strand of its development at least, a reaction against the speculative idealism of Hegel. (Though, on the other hand, one should notice, Sartre at least takes a great deal from Hegel.) But it is, again, only in a very vague and ambiguous sense that nineteenth-century philosophy in general, from Schelling to Nietzsche, can be labeled "existential." This is, after all, a fairly definite historical movement in philosophy, taking its name from Kierkegaard's phrase "existential dialectic." Kierkegaard, it is true, was himself a nineteenth-century philosopher, influenced by Schelling and, more deeply than he would himself have granted, even by the archfiend Hegel. But Kierkegaard was in his own time completely without fame or influence; and to spread the name of his peculiar brand of dialectic over an indefinite number of his predecessors and contemporaries is to spread it very thin.

Moreover, as Sartre and numerous others have repeatedly insisted, there is, in fact, no need for all this vagueness and obscurity, since an extremely simple, literal, and precise definition of existential philosophy is easy to come by and easy to remember. Existentialism is the philosophy which declares as its first principle that existence is prior to essence. This is, presumably, a technically accurate principle, yet as simple and intelligible as "2 and 2 are 4." Why, then, all the bewilderment about the philosophy that follows from it? "Existence is prior to essence." It is as easy as that. Of course, to understand the principle and apply it properly, one must make at least one very important qualification. Taking literally the simple assertion, "Existence is prior to essence," one

[2]

might find existentialists in very unexpected quarters. For instance, in the thirteenth-century controversy about proofs of the existence of God, the Augustinians believed in the priority of essence to existence—in the possibility of moving from the idea of God, the intuitive apprehension of His essence (in so far as such apprehension of the infinite is possible to finite minds), to the assertion of his existence. Their opponents, the Christian Aristotelians, on the contrary, believed in the priority, at least for the genesis of human knowledge, of existence to essence—in the necessity of starting with the givens of our sensuous experience and proceeding by induction and abstraction to the ultimate intuitive awareness of essences and eternal truths.[1] Yet, if there is anyone in the whole of Western philosophy who has never been accused of being an existentialist, surely it is St. Thomas!

The necessary qualification to the existentialist principle easily appears, however, if we look at Kierkegaard's original critique of Hegelian philosophy. The "logic" of Hegel "moves" in its ponderous way from being and essence to actuality and existence—or, rather, from being and essence, through existence, to the higher synthesis of both in Mind (Geist) or Concept (Begriff). But for Kierkegaard, as we shall see, the whole notion of starting with "pure being" and of moving from it to existence is absurd. Out of pure logic, pure thought, can come no movement of any sort, for movement implies change, time, nonbeing. Least of all can pure thought produce the movement of emergence into actuality, into the hard, resistant, senseless fact of what is, forever distinct from the conveniently definable nature of what might be. The Hegelian play with essences is a pompous, professorial game, great in pretensions but despicably trivial in its basic reality. But the existence to which Kierkegaard contrasts

1. Existence is prior to essence in St. Thomas only in the order of knowing, not of being; but the example is sufficient to show that the general principle, simply stated, does not hold. Existentialism is not *the* philosophy for which, in general, existence is prior to essence.

this game with essences, the sheer fact that summons him from the dream-world of speculation, is, nearly always, a very particular existence: that of the thinker himself who plays the game. How pitiable is the wretched Hegelian professor, building his great dream-palace and living beside it in a hovel; marching with the World-soul through China and India but neglecting, until it shrivels up to nothing, the only soul that should really concern him—his own. It is fact, indeed, that existentialism puts before essence—but a particular human fact. Not the sense-perceptions of a Thomas, generally accessible in their standard character to all our species, not even the more "subjective" but equally uniform impressions of Hume, but just the unique, inexpressible that of any one conscious being's particular existence—such is the actuality that Kierkegaard and his twentieth-century successors agree in referring to when they declare, as their first principle, the priority of existence over essence.

2

Taking existentialism, however, in the context of reactions against Hegel and the peculiar "absolute idealism" derived from him, one may, of course, insist that the movement has in this respect no uniqueness, that the pragmatism of James and Dewey, for example, was an equally effective and much less outlandish rebellion against the once omnipresent Hegelians. There is certainly, in James, a similar turning of the philosopher's attention from speculative system-building to more pressing human concerns: "The stagnant felicity of the Absolute's own perfection moves me as little as I move it." There is even, at some points, a distinct likeness between the pragmatic description of knowledge and the contemporary existentialists' analysis of human experience. For example, there is the well-known description by Heidegger of the function of the "sign" in our everyday experience. Things in our world occur primarily not as indifferently *there*, like Cartesian extended substances, but as things "at hand," things there *for* this or that use. Among the things-at-hand, among the shoes and ships and sealing wax, are a class of things that point, and notably things that point as signs. These signs—for instance, in Heidegger's example, the mechanical hand on German buses that showed the direction that the bus was going to turn—are themselves things-at-hand, with the same function of being there *for* something as other things have. Their differentia is that, as signs pointing to other things, they not only serve a particular practical use but reveal something of the relations between things and therefore of the nature of things-at-hand in general—still, however, things-*at-hand*, interpreted as useful for something not as merely there. Thus signs are doubly pragmatic. First, they are only one class in a universe of things pragmatically interpreted, things-for-use. Second, the use which they have is to subserve a pragmatic interpretation of the world: to illuminate the general structure of the world in which we live as itself constituted by things-for-use and our use of or concern with them. Within this class of sign-pragmata, moreover, symbol, expression, and meaning are themselves only subclasses, listed along with "trace, remains, memorial, document, evidence, appearance."[2] All this looks very like a variation of James's theme of ideas as railroad tickets from one station to another in our experience, or like a differently oriented but not basically dissimilar version of Dewey's experimental logic. In fact, a detailed comparison of Heidegger and Dewey has been attempted at least once; and a superficial likeness one certainly cannot deny.

2. Martin Heidegger, *Sein und Zeit, erste Hälfte* (Halle: Max Niemeyer, 1931). First published in 1927.

[5]

Even in Sartre, though he decries the pragmatic theory of knowledge as "pure subjective idealism," one can find statements which are, though much more complex and subtle than anything in the Jamesian or Deweyan philosophies, not out of harmony, at any rate, with the general tenor of the pragmatic account of knowing as subordinate to doing. There is a striking passage, for example, in an article on "Materialism and Revolution" in *Les Temps modernes*. The theme of the essay—the revolutionary as existentialist, not as materialist (of which we shall have more to say in a later chapter)—would doubtless shock the innate conservatism of an orthodox pragmatist. But Sartre's statement of the intrinsic relation between human ends and the perception of nonhuman, mechanical cause-and-effect patterns is, if not pragmatic, something the pragmatists *should* have said if they had known what they were at:

Here again materialism gives the revolutionary more than he asks. For the revolutionary demands not to be a thing but to govern things. It is true that he has acquired, in work, a correct appreciation of freedom. That [freedom] which has been mirrored for him by his action on things is far removed from the abstract freedom of thought of the Stoic. It manifests itself in a particular situation into which the worker has been thrown by the chance of his birth and the caprice or interest of his master. It appears in an enterprise which he has not started of his own free will and which he will not finish; it is not distinguishable from his very engagement at the heart of that enterprise; but, finally, if he becomes aware of his freedom, from the depth of his slavery, it is because he measures the efficacy of his concrete action. He does not have the pure idea of an autonomy that he does not enjoy, but he knows his power, which is proportionate to his action. What he establishes, in the course of the action itself, is that he goes beyond [*dépasse*] the present state of the material by a precise project of disposing of it in such and such a way and that, this project being identical with the government of means in view of ends, he, in fact, succeeds in disposing of it as he wished. If he discovers the relation of cause to effect, it is

[6]

not in submitting to it, but in the very act which goes beyond the present state (adherence of coal to the walls of the mine, etc.), but toward a certain end which, from the depth of the future, illuminates and defines that state. Thus the relation of cause to effect is revealed in and by the efficacy of an act which is at once project and realization. It is, in fact, the docility and at the same time the resistance of the universe which show him at the same time the constancy of causal series and the image of his liberty; for the fact is that his liberty is indistinguishable from the utilization of causal series for an end which it itself sets. Without the illumination which that end provides for the present situation, there would be in that situation neither causal connection nor relation of means to end, or rather there would be an indistinct infinity of means and ends, of effects and causes, just as there would be an undifferentiated infinity of circles, ellipses, triangles, and polygons in geometric space, without the generative act of the mathematician who traces a figure by binding a series of points chosen according to a certain law. Thus, in work, determinism does not reveal freedom in so far as it is an abstract law of nature but in so far as a human project carves out and illuminates, in the midst of the infinite interaction of phenomena, a certain partial determinism. And, in this determinism, which is proved simply by the efficacy of human action—as the principle of Archimedes was already used and understood by shipbuilders long before Archimedes had given it its conceptual form—the relation of cause to effect is indiscernible from that of means to end. The organic unity of the project of the worker is the emergence of an end which at first was not in the universe and which manifests itself by the disposition of means with a view to achieving it (for the end is nothing but the synthetic unity of all the means arranged to produce it); and, at the same time, the lower stratum, which subtends these means and is discovered in its turn by their very disposition, is the relation of cause to effect: like the principle of Archimedes, at once support and content of the technique of shipbuilders. In this sense, one can say that the atom was created by the atomic bomb, which is conceived only in the light of the Anglo-American project of winning a war. Thus freedom is discovered only in the act, is one with the act; it is the foundation of the connections and interactions which constitute the internal structure of the act; it never is enjoyed but is revealed in and by its products; it is not an inner power of snatching one's self out of the most urgent situations, for there is no outside or inside for man. But it exists, on the contrary, for engaging one's self in present action and constructing a future; it is that by which there is born a future which permits understanding and changing the present. Thus the worker, in fact, learns his freedom from things, but precisely because the things teach him that he is anything in the world but a thing.[3]

In the same article, too, Sartre gives an account of the genesis of philosophic systems not unlike Dewey's description, for instance, in *Reconstruction in Philosophy*. Philosophies have in the past, according to both authors, served the function of stabilizing the norms by which the ruling class in a society justifies itself; their pretensions to intellectual objectivity or to universal truth have been, in fact, the pretensions of the privileged to self-perpetuation. Sartre's language is in the tradition of Marx rather than in the Humian line, from which Dewey's talk of custom, habit, and so on appears to stem; but their accounts of the social origin of what purports to be pure speculation are certainly similar. As against such false hypostatization of ideas or ideals, moreover, both of them would in a sense turn the direction of values from past to future: from a crystallization of what has been to an aspiration toward what needs to be. "What, then, in reality, is a value," says Sartre, "if not the call of that which is not yet?"[4] True, one might say it is present more than future that Dewey turns to (see his denunciation of the utilitarians' "hedonistic calculus" because of its exclusive direction to future things wanted rather than to interests and satisfactions felt now). A more important difference, however, in the two accounts lies not in Dewey's lesser emphasis on the future but in the *kind* of future to

3. Jean-Paul Sartre, "Matérialisme et révolution (fin)," *Les Temps modernes*, I, No. 10 (July, 1946), 18–20.
4. *Ibid.*, p. 12.

which each writer wants to shift our attention. To turn values from past to future is for Sartre to turn from the sanctioning of bourgeois privilege to a vision that sees beyond the sectional interests of the society and hence to revolution. For Dewey the change from what were falsely called "eternal principles" of truth and morals is to a sort of spontaneous growth of progressive democracy. Sartre's solution implies, as far as I can see, a philosophy of perpetual revolution. Dewey's, seeing beyond the segments of a past society but remaining faithfully within the present one, provides something like a new dogmatism, less precise in outline but just as dogmatic as those it replaces.

Such differences within their similarities suggest, moreover, a difference much more fundamental than any likeness. For one thing, pragmatism, with its admiration for science and scientific method, in turning philosophic emphasis from the speculative to the factual, from universal to particular, turns more generally than existentialism to facts as such, to the stream of perceptions, in themselves humanly indifferent, which follow continuously through our consciousness and even, by some accounts, constitute it. Pragmatism in this regard continues, though in a different style, the heritage of Locke and Hume, while existentialism substitutes a new and puzzling concrete givenness for the indifferent outer flow of sense-data that constitutes the material for scientific construction. Therefore, it is a different kind of existence whose priority to essence is proclaimed by the two philosophies.

Nor is that yet the most significant difference between them. What is really essential is not so much the kind of fact each stresses as the relation between fact and value envisaged by the two schools. After a fine, "scientific," "tough-minded" account of the democratic man's liberation from false traditional moralities there always comes, in Dewey and his followers, a point at which one suddenly finds that, with the elimination of religious superstition and metaphysical ignorance, new values or even old ones have been spontaneously generated out of the bedrock of fact and more fact. So from habit suddenly comes "intelligent habit," from impulses grow "integrated" impulses, from each man's interest in his own activity here and now comes the glorious growth of a harmonious society in which all work willingly and sweetly together for the good of all. And at that point pragmatism itself succumbs to a delusion at least as grievous as those by which Hegel's pure speculants deceived themselves; for mere facts will never to all eternity generate values; nor can science—psychology as little as nuclear physics—by itself generate either good or evil. Not, as Sartre points out in the article already quoted, the mechanical interconnections of things but the free acts of men upon those things create, maintain, and constitute values. It is in the dichotomy between fact and value, between what merely and irrationally but undeniably is, and what we aspire to, yet what as undeniably is not: in what Ibsen's Brand calls "the darkly felt split between things as they are and things as they ought to be," that human greatness as well as human failure lies. And it is the perception of that dichotomy that is the central and significant insight of existential philosophy. As against such insight, pragmatism appears rather as giving only the reverse side of Palmström's dictum in the Morgenstern ballad:

> Weil, so schloss er messerscharf,
> Nicht sein kann was nicht sein darf.[5]

The inadequacy of scientifically oriented philosophies to explain the genesis of values is more conspicuous perhaps,

5. "For, he concludes, razor-keen,
What's not supposed to be cannot be."

though not essentially different, in the position of the school now variously called "logical positivism," "scientific empiricism," or the like; for here the emphasis on modern logistic methods, on the one hand, and, on the other, the explicit restriction of the "facts" that logic or mathematics works on, to spatiotemporally locatable sense-data have doubly removed the subject matter of philosophy from any relevance to the felt reality of the individual consciousness. But it is, for the existentialist, only within the confines of that reality, unwillingly flung into its world, yet freely making a world of it, that good and evil, importance and unimportance, can originate. Values are created, in other words, only by the free act of a human agent who *takes* this or that to be good or bad, beautiful or ugly, in the light of his endeavor to give significance and order to an otherwise meaningless world. Now positivistic ethics is, as it vaunts itself to be, descriptive, not normative; it describes men's value-judgments as behavioristic psychology described the paths of rats in mazes. And, although such descriptions may be detailed and accurate, they have, from an existentialist point of view, little to do with the problems of morality—as little as the positivist's manipulations of artificial symbol-systems have to do with the infinite shades and subtleties of meaning of what are deprecatingly called "natural languages." Whatever the shortcomings of his Puritan fanaticism, in one respect at least Kant's ethics was undeniably correct: there is no good or evil apart from will—and there is, for the existentialist as for Kant, no will apart from freedom. But for positivism there are only two necessities: mathematical and mechanical; or rather, more strictly speaking, there are only, on one side, the empty necessity of logic and, on the other, the compulsion of chance which establishes, statistically, a kind of pseudo-necessity. Freedom there certainly is not, except as the nonsensical babbling of philosophers. Such an orienta-

[11]

tion in fact or in existence, then, is as much the contrary of existentialism as is the systematic idealism that they both oppose.

3

Existentialism does not, then, turn to existence in the sense that it finds human values emergent from mere facts, as pragmatism or positivism try to do. It is a reaction as much against the claims of scientific philosophies as it is against the more high-sounding but no more ambitious systems that preceded them. But in that case one may wonder how existentialism differs from other contemporary movements that claim to redeem a lost humanity by rescuing us from, not through, science. There are, notably, two directions for such revolt against the intellectual and spiritual predominance of the scientific temper. One may demand, like Reinhold Niebuhr, a return to Christian faith; or one may rely, as, for example, such writers as Brand Blanshard or R. M. Hutchins variously do, on truths of reason accessible to all who are willing to understand them. As distinct from the simple naïveté of pragmatist and positivist, what all these writers have to say *against* our faith, our philosophy, our education, or our political unwisdom is entirely convincing. But against both sorts of remedy—the religious and the metaphysical— there are at least two objections in the light of which existentialism appears, at any rate, a plausible alternative.

In the first place, one can take it as given that this is, in the sense of traditional Christianity, a faithless generation. But simply to assert to such a generation that faith is what it needs is—even should it be true faith—to talk, like Zarathustra, to a deaf and unheeding multitude: "this is not the mouth for these ears." Faith is not to be had by fiat but only by much more devious and difficult, and certainly unpredictable, ways. And the same holds for metaphysical "knowledge," which is—Blanshard's brilliant expositions to the con-

[12]

trary notwithstanding—as deeply based on faith as is any supernatural knowledge. The framers of our Constitution conceived, some of them at any rate, that they were founding a government on the eternal truths of reason. To us who have lost the Newtonian-Lockean scientific basis for their principles, our belief in those same principles has become an act of faith, not an insight of reason—of faith in reason itself, perhaps—but nevertheless an act by which we believe, not an argument by which we know. The world-views, whether Thomistic or Cartesian, in the light of which these truths could be demonstrated and conveyed like mathematical theorems to docile pupils, are dead and gone; and, however deeply we may believe in the doctrine of the brotherhood of man, we can neither prove its universal truth nor persuade if we could prove.

That is not a specifically existentialist objection. And, of course, for some existentialists, like the Catholic Marcel (or in a very different sense for the first existentialist, Kierkegaard) a return to faith in a Christian God is a possible and even necessary way out of our present moral chaos. What an atheistic existentialist like Sartre asserts, however, of either the religious or the metaphysical solution is that we have here only another endeavor, like the positivistic and as fruitless, to found values not in free human actions but in objective facts. True, the facts this time are not sense-data but supernatural mysteries or eternal truths of reason. Yet they still are facts, which we discover existing objectively outside ourselves and on which we can rely, in blissful dependence, to guide our actions toward the good and the right. So both these attitudes, equally with materialistic or positivistic theories, exemplify what Sartre calls "the spirit of seriousness": they seek to escape our ultimate, inexplicable, and terrible responsibility for the values that we live by, by giving them a cosmic rather than a human, a necessary rather than a libertarian, source.

[13]

How existentialism fares in its endeavor to save us at once from all these false idols we shall try, in the succeeding chapters, to discover. We shall find in it, I think—in some of its proponents at least—a brilliant statement of the tragic dilemma if not of man, at least of man in our time. And we shall find in it, also, relentless, even extravagant, honesty in the rejection of easy solutions or apparent solutions to that dilemma. Whether such honesty itself, heroically maintained against every intellectual temptation, can in its splendid, self-righteous isolation, of its own force prove the solution of its own problem—that is at first, and perhaps will be to the end, an open question.

CHAPTER TWO

SØREN KIERKEGAARD: THE SELF
AGAINST THE SYSTEM

1

A THINKER who hates the abstract complexity of metaphysical systems, yet whose thought is persistently, in
fact, systematically, directed to working through a
single all-important problem—such a thinker's work should
be relatively easy to summarize or evaluate. But Kierkegaard's one problem was so specifically religious in character and so complex in its literary presentation (complex
out of all proportion to its philosophic scope) that to assess
it philosophically is a difficult task indeed. In the light of
Kierkegaard's growing influence, however, the task must be
attempted—and that despite the obvious fact that Kierkegaard himself would have considered it irrelevant and impossible. A philosophic, as distinct from a literary or religious,
assessment? Fantastic! Any assessment by anyone except that
rare person whom Kierkegaard calls "his reader" (and I
confess, thankfully I fear, I am not he)? Fantastic again!
Yet one must try to make something of this apparently stim-
ulating, certainly irritating, figure; and if the attempt itself
is absurd, that at least might have pleased the apostle of
absurdity.[1]

Kierkegaard's problem, as he puts it in the *Philosophical
Fragments*, was "to find out where the misunderstanding lies
between speculation and Christianity." It is, he believes, in
the nature of personal existence that this misunderstanding
has its roots; and so his thought centers in the problem of the

---

1. For some accounts of Kierkegaard's life see Bibliographical Note, p. 150.

individual and his personal or subjective existence, his existence as "inwardness"; that is what speculation overlooks or radically misinterprets, and that is what the approach to Christian truth requires that one understand. "Subjectivity," then, is what Kierkegaard sets himself to think about; but his view of it is never divorced from the problem of Christian faith and seldom from the task of refuting speculative error. So the statement of the *Fragments* seems a fair one to take as fundamental. If it be so taken, however, Kierkegaard's thought must be considered as determined by his conception, on the one hand, of speculation and, on the other, of Christianity.

2

By "speculation" Kierkegaard means Hegelian speculation. That is not to deny that he sometimes contrasts the insight sought by the subjective thinker with the empty objectivity of sensory and historical knowledge, as well as with philosophic (i.e., Hegelian) speculation. One can find in the *Papers*, for instance, a strong indictment of empirical science—in particular, physiology, as applied to the human species:

In our time it is especially the natural sciences which are dangerous. Physiology will at last spread so that it will take ethics along. There are already traces enough of a new tendency—to treat ethics like physics: whereby all of ethics becomes illusion, and the ethical element in the race comes to be treated statistically with averages, or to be reckoned as one reckons oscillations in natural laws. A physiologist takes it upon himself to explain the whole person. Here the question is: *principiis obsta*: what shall I do with it? What need have I to know about the centripetal and centrifugal circulation of nerves, about the blood stream, about the human being's microscopic state *in utero*? *Ethics has tasks enough for me.* Or do I need to know how digestion works in order to be able to eat? Or do I need to know how the movement in the nervous system works—in order to believe in God and love men? And if someone should say, "True, for that one certainly does not need it," then I should ask again: "But what if it weakens all my ethical passion, that I become an observer of nature? What if, with the whole manifold knowledge of analogies, of abnormalities, of this and that, I lose more and more the impression of the ethical: *thou shalt, it is thou, thou hast nothing to do with a single other person, though heaven and earth collapse* THOU SHALT? What if [to pursue that knowledge] is to provide myself with a lot of sneaking evasions and excuses? Suppose it is turning my attention away from what is important to let myself begin on physiology, instead of letting physiology go and saying: 'Begin.' "[2]

Such a passage is perhaps more characteristic for the existential movement generally, considered in its negative aspect as a revolt against the characteristic intellectual temper of our age, than are Kierkegaard's more specific attacks on the Hegelian brand of objectivity. But though a more general antiscientific revolt may be considered a legitimate inference from Kierkegaard's position, his acquaintance with scientific achievement of any degree of sophistication or precision was so extremely slight and his attention to it, even negatively, so infrequent that one must regard his own problem, whatever its more general implications, as bounded, in the main, by the Hegelian tradition.

Within these limits Kierkegaard certainly ranks among the outstanding critics of Hegel and Hegelianism or perhaps, by implication, of ontology as such. Such criticisms are constantly recurrent throughout the works and papers.

One finds again and again, for example, the objection that the System is *sub specie aeternitatis*, whereas existence is temporal. Similarly, the System is no system unless it is finished (and has thus attained to a timeless state), whereas existence while existing is never finished—and the System is thus incapable of accounting for existence. This incompat-

2. Søren Kierkegaard, *Papirer*, ed. P. A. Heiberg, V. Kuhr, and E. Torsting (Copenhagen, 1909——), Vol. VII, Part I, Div. A, No. 182 (referred to hereafter as "*P*").

ibility Kierkegaard stresses, for example, in his criticisms of the concept of "movement" in logic. It is implied in his gibes at the System for never attaining the state of systematic completion that it promises:

> I am willing to fall down adoringly before the System, if only I can catch sight of it. Until now I have not succeeded in so doing; and, although I have young legs, still I am almost tired of running from Herod to Pilate. Several times I have been quite near to adoration; but lo, at the moment when I had already spread out my handkerchief in order not to soil my trousers in kneeling; when for the last time I guilelessly said to one of the initiate, "Now tell me honestly, is it really quite finished? For in that case I shall prostrate myself, even though I should ruin a pair of trousers"—for by reason of the heavy traffic to and from the System the path is not a little soiled—I always got the answer: "No, as yet it is, in fact, not quite completed." And so it was postponed again—both the System and the kneeling.[3]

The fantastic claims of the System over against existence are shown up again by Kierkegaard's theory of the leap. The "absolute beginning" becomes, if we observe the process of thought honestly, an illusion. The beginning of philosophy, like any other action, has, in Kierkegaard's view, a specific factual setting; and it manifests the radical discontinuity characteristic of the commencement of every intellectual as well as moral process: it begins not from "pure Being" or any such nonsense but from a sudden flash of understanding, best described as a "leap." "Who has forgotten," Kierkegaard asks the Danish Hegelians, "the lovely Easter morning when Professor Heiberg arose to understand the Hegelian philosophy; as he himself has so inspiringly explained it— was not that a leap? Or was there someone who had dreamed about it?"[4]

Or the unreality of the Hegelian procedure is pointed,

3. Søren Kierkegaard, *Samlede Vaerker*, ed. A. B. Drachmann, I. L. Heiberg, and H. O. Lange (2d ed.; Copenhagen, 1920–31), VII, 95 (referred to hereafter as "S").
4. *P*, *V*, *C*, 3.

as was mentioned in the previous chapter, by reference to the life of the philosopher himself in relation to his system. "Most systematizers in relation to their system fare," he says, "like the man who builds a huge palace and himself lives next door to it in a barn."[5] He never tires of contrasting the "little dingle-dangle of an existing Herr Professor who writes the system"[6] to his grandiose metaphysical edifice, and ridiculing the implicit reduction of the speculant's own existence to abstraction, which the practice of Hegelian philosophy seems to him to involve. "A philosopher," he says, "has gradually become such a fantastic creature that the wildest imagination has scarcely invented anything so fabulous";[7] for by the understanding "of China and Persia," he believes, one is not helped but rather hindered in that understanding of one's self which is for him the only important understanding.

Kierkegaard suggests some of the methods by which the systematic hoax succeeds. It illegitimately introduces predicates of value into logical arguments. What is "bad infinity" for instance? "Is bad a dialectical determination? How do scorn and contempt and means of terrorization find a place as admissible propelling forces in logic?"[8] Moreover, the Hegelian method guides the student through transitions apparently logical, but actually verbal only. Of this ruse he gives as an example the play on "Wesen/gewesen": "*Wesen ist, was ist gewesen; ist gewesen* is a *tempus praeteritum* of *sein* ['being'] therefore *Wesen* is '*das aufgehobene Sein* ["suspended being"],' the *Sein* that has been. That is a logical movement!"[9] The System deceives, finally, by the grand vistas that it displays. It draws attention from the more humble problems which, in Kierkegaard's opinion, properly concern the finite knower, to dizzying processions of the

5. *Ibid.*, VII, 1, A, 82.
6. *S*, VII, 110.
7. *Ibid.*, VII, 105.
8. *Ibid.*, VII, 101.
9. *Ibid.*, IV, 316 n.

world-mind, persuading the student that, in comparison with "6,000 years of world-history,"[10] his own small existence is of no importance. The absolute method is, for the moralist Kierkegaard, "a bad conscience in purple."[11]

Danish philosophy, should such an entity come into being, is to have a very different temper:

> Danish philosophy, if there can some day be talk of such a thing, will differ in this respect from the German, that it will not begin with nothing, or without all presupposition, nor explain everything by mediating; but, on the contrary, it will begin with the proposition: that there are many things between heaven and earth which no philosopher has explained. That proposition will, by its admittance into philosophy, furnish the proper corrective, and at the same time cast a humorous-edifying agitation over the whole.[12]

3

In fact, of course, that thing between heaven and earth which concerns Danish philosophy in the person of Kierkegaard is the Christian paradox, whether considered as the paradox of the God-man or as the paradox of the human individual's faith—that is, his experience of nothingness before God which is yet the fulfilment of his existence. So Kierkegaard's philosophizing, bounded on the one side by the Hegelian tradition, is limited on the other side by the constant presence of Christian faith (a "limit," of course, only for the non-Christian, but as such it must appear in a general philosophic account of Kierkegaard). It is through that presence, Kierkegaard himself says, that his dialectic "goes further than Socrates":

> This project indisputably goes further than the Socratic, as is evident at every point. Whether it is therefore truer than the Socratic is an entirely different question, which cannot be decided in the same breath, for here there was assumed a new

10. *Ibid.*, VII, 107.
11. *P, V, B,* 41.   12. *Ibid.*, V, A, 46.

organ—faith; and a new presupposition—the consciousness of sin; a new decision—the moment; and a new teacher—God in time. . . . .[13]

And his thought is further limited by his own peculiar conception of Christianity, which not only does not correspond exactly to any Christian orthodoxy at least up to his own day but eliminates altogether, according to the account of the *Fragments* and the *Unscientific Postscript*, any conception of an "objective truth of Christianity." The whole problem for every serious Christian, according to Kierkegaard, lies on the subjective side, in the riddle of his own path to faith. Not the understanding of any general relation of man to God, not the building of any elaborate theological edifice, but the way to eternal blessedness for "my own little I" is every Christian's whole concern. But that means, for Kierkegaard, turning sharply away from systematization and objectivity to subjectivity, to "inwardness," as Kierkegaard likes to call it. It means turning from the "extensive" life of unexamined sensation to the "intensive" life of introspection. It means turning from the knowledge of general, abstract, and therefore nonreal propositions to some sort of noncognitive grasp (sometimes called "essential knowledge," but most unlike knowledge in any commonly understood sense of that word) of the particular, concrete, real existent: that is, of the individual himself, who is the only real existent for himself, except for the infinite being whom he comes to acknowledge through faith. It means, in a word, turning from tautology to paradox: from systems of impersonal "truth" that are, because impersonal, as superficial and trivial as they are consistent, to the one passionately realized subjective truth that is profoundly meaningful because it is profoundly self-contradictory—because it is absurd from start to finish; for to cleave to subjectivity is for Kierkegaard to reject all abstraction, even so much as is necessary for the imaginative

13. S., IV, 302.

[21]

transference through words of my experience into yours. But seriously to reject all abstraction is to renounce the whole sphere of logic and consistency and to leave only contradiction and its linguistic expression, paradox. Hence paradox is the tool of Kierkegaard's "indirect communication"; and contradiction the defining character, for him, of consciousness itself: "Immediacy is reality, language is ideality, consciousness is contradiction. The moment I pronounce reality, contradiction is there, for what I say is ideality."[14]

It is, then, to personal existence and to the absurd, the self-contradictory, the radically incommunicable in personal existence that the anti-Hegelian, Christian thinker has to turn; and it is this passionate attention to the inwardness of personal existence, it is this "infinite interest," as Kierkegaard calls it, in one's single isolated self, together with the emphasis on paradox that the accompanying denial of all generality or abstraction appears to involve, that determines the peculiar quality of his thought. First, last, and always his thought is directed, within the double boundary of the refutation of Hegelian error and the approach to Christian truth, to a single question: "What is the self that remains if a person has lost the whole world and yet not lost himself?"[15]

14. *P*, IV, B, 145. In its barest logical form the situation is simply stated. Either as "speculant" one seeks "objective truth," which is reducible to tautology, i.e., to the form "a or non-a" or its equivalent "not both a and non-a." Or as Christian thinker one seeks subjectivity, i.e., one denies objectivity and therewith the logical principle of objectivity and asserts "both a and non-a," which is contradiction or paradox. So, for example, contradiction is the limiting-point of the dialectic of *Either-Or*, the expression of the aesthetic stage of personal existence. This kind of life corresponds concretely, Kierkegaard comments in the *Papers* (*P*, III, B, 177) to the intellectual deification of tautology; for "everywhere," he says, the dialectic of *Either-Or* "leads everything to the dilemma." Or, as he puts it in *Either-Or* (*S*, I, 26): "Hang yourself, you will regret it; do not hang yourself, you will also regret it; hang yourself or do not hang yourself, you will regret both. That, gentlemen, is the summation of human wisdom." How can one escape from this series of meaningless alternatives? Only by a complete about-face from the objective to the subjective, which implies the denial of the supreme principle of objectivity, i.e., the denial of the law of contradiction.

15. *P*, IV, C, 77.

4

The character of that question and the sense in which attention to it genuinely involves a new direction in philosophy may be clarified by some brief historical comments.

a) Kant's revolution in philosophy involved the focusing of philosophic investigation on the question What is man? with its three subdivisions, What can I know? What ought I to do? and What may I hope? Kierkegaard shares the Kantian conviction that philosophy deals with human problems, that it can consider only the nature of our limited powers of knowing or doing, not the essence of some vast cosmic reality. Within the analysis of knowledge, too, Kierkegaard shares the Kantian view of the separation of thought and being, essence and existence (his theory of knowledge, as a matter of fact, is more like Hume's than like Kant's, more like some modern positivisms than like either). But Kant's treatment of human nature, though it denies our reason the power to deduce the universe, leaves it unity and completeness enough in the deduction of itself. It was the one system of reason that Kant hoped to have described: a reason everywhere unified even in its diversifications—where thought supplements intuition, reason supplements understanding, will supplements intellect, and the whole is one eternally valid structure of the human mind. For Kierkegaard, however, there is no such one totality of human nature which could be directly and systematically described. There are just these human existences, whose inner quality the subjective thinker can attempt to communicate only by the most devious sorts of indirection. It is, much more concretely, the "modes of human reality," as Jaspers calls them, that Kierkegaard wants to interpret—the variations of human personality as they *feel* to the person himself; the development of human personalities caught in the very flux of time, where eternity enters as standard or ideal but not as system. For Kant the thing in itself is beyond our knowledge, even the

I itself; but human reason in its functioning is clear, open, intelligible to the reasoning mind; once the cleansing tool of criticism has been used, reason can be once for all described in all the beauty of its complex organic structure. But for Kierkegaard the question What is man? has no such systematic answer. He makes much of Socrates' statement in the opening of the *Phaedrus*: that he may himself be a monster stranger than Typhon, that he must therefore devote himself to the quest of his own nature as of something infinitely important but strange, puzzling, and full of mystery. Not man as such, but the strange, inaccessible self who remains when a person has lost the whole world but not himself, the very real inner impassioned feel of self, the self beyond the transcendental unity, which for Kant is unknowable and incommunicable—that is Kierkegaard's concern. And in that attention to the inner feeling of the person in its completely concrete qualitative reality, Kierkegaard is turning aside not only from the Kantian kind of *Vernunft-system* but from the main stream of Western philosophy since Aristotle; for, after all, if one really stops to think about it, one must admit that, with the possible exception of such antiphilosophical philosophers as Pascal, most philosophers have treated the nature of man in a fashion whose abstraction and unreality is quite staggering. If, for example, the saintly vision of a Spinoza makes of human reason a power it does not in this evil world in fact possess, consider even the so-called "empirical" philosophies: the atomism of the ancients or the associationism of the British tradition, which thought themselves close to good, honest, obvious things. Consider their conception of human life as put together of distinct little bits of red, round, sweet, hard, pleasant, painful, etc. Try really to take it literally, even for a moment. Surely it is fantastically apart from what concretely, in its vague half-meaningless confusion of something and nothing, of direction and indirection, our experience at most times is.

b) It may be significant, moreover, that, in turning aside from an abstract philosophic tradition to something closer to the inner feeling of our experience (from quantity to quality, as he would say), Kierkegaard so frequently and explicitly turns back to the Socrates of the dialogues. Platonic influences, in the sense of a Neo-Platonic tradition, one may, of course, find everywhere in Western thought. But in Kierkegaard one finds something much rarer: a genuine return to the dialogues themselves as to a fresh source of philosophic insight, a return like that of Castiglione's *Courtier;* and Kierkegaard, like Castiglione, draws heavily on the *Symposium.* It is not to Plato's doctrine—for to understand that is always to misunderstand Plato—but to the Platonic Socrates, so strangely identified with philosophy itself, that Kierkegaard goes. He has, as far as I remember, nothing much to say about the theory of ideas, about levels of being, or any such elaborate "Platonic" cosmological schemata; but he knew the dialogues and loved them, I suspect, with a passion truly akin to the *theia mania* of the *Phaedrus.* Tortured and twisted as his thinking is, it shares with Renaissance Platonism a genuine reverence for Plato—or Plato's Socrates—as the fountainhead of philosophic wisdom. In Kierkegaard, of course, Christian faith enters as contrast rather than as complement to the Socratic situation: the aim of the *Fragments* is to solve the Socratic problem of learning by means that are radically different from Plato's—different just because of the interposition of Christianity. So there is here no easy fusion between Plato and Christianity. Yet in Kierkegaard as in Renaissance Platonists the turn from a later tradition to the Platonic dialogues is oddly linked with a deep revitalization in philosophy—a sense of turning from the dry bones of technical systems to thoughts still living,

[25]

through Plato's art, in the person of his teacher. Were it not for the signal exception of Bergson, I should almost feel inclined to take the philosophic revolt of our own day—for instance, in Whitehead—as a further instance of the way in which a rebirth of philosophy means a return to Plato, a sort of historical recollection, if you like. But, apart from any such tempting generalizations, one may certainly feel in Kierkegaard himself an uncanny directness in his dealing with the dialogues and a tremendous power in the insight he draws from them. Whatever historical analogies one draws or does not draw, this is, within narrow range, indeed, but still quite genuinely, a little renaissance, occurring oddly in the dreary nineteenth century but growing in significance as that dreariness in our own day becomes despair.

5

It may be said, of course, that it is unnecessary to go back to Kierkegaard for a new impulse in philosophy, that such a movement as pragmatism, as we suggested earlier, has already effected what existential philosophy aims at—that is, it has rebelled against the arid technicality of metaphysics and has brought philosophy closer to the living problems of real people. The sense in which pragmatism fails to accomplish at least the second of these aims and the sense in which Kierkegaard points at least to a direction more appropriate for dealing with them may be indicated by an example, slight in itself but suggestive of a larger contrast. Death is certainly an important fact in every man's life; look at the way in which Kierkegaard and a pragmatist like Dewey treat it. In the course of his argument against the traditional means-end conception in *Human Nature and Conduct*, Dewey analyzes the situation of a man building a house. The man is not building the house in order to live in it, Dewey says, for he might die before it was finished; so he is building it for the sake of the present activity itself. Compare this

[26]

glancing reference to the continual imminence of death with Kierkegaard's conception of the way in which death constantly determines or should determine the manner of our lives. The conception of "being glad over 70,000 fathoms," of living constantly in the face of death, in the awareness that here and now may be the last moment—that is for Kierkegaard, as for contemporary existentialism, a central and terribly serious motif in the interpretation of human life. I am not sure whether "das Sein zum Tode" is really the fundamental determinant in our experience, pushed back but never canceled by the trivializing demands of every day; or whether, though recurring conspicuously at moments in our lives, it assumes an all-important place only in certain situations—such situations as the underground movements, a main source of French existentialism, had to face. In either case death and the dread of death do at least form a recurrent thread in human life, a thread sufficiently conspicuous that a philosophic account of man's nature needs to take serious notice of it. Yet in Dewey's argument the conception of death is something to be toyed with as a convenient logical device for refuting somebody else's theory of something else. That is but one example, of course, but it illustrates well, I think, the limitations of the pragmatic movement as a philosophic rebellion. Pragmatism was directed against a number of things, but it contained nothing positive beyond the pleasant desire to make things comfortable. Whatever is uncomfortable— death, sin, despair—it passes by on the other side. As has been said a number of times, pragmatism is afraid to face evil.[16] And it is afraid, too, to face the ultimate puzzle of human individuality. To be sure, the individual and the activities of the individual are what pragmatism, like existential philosophy, is supposed to devote itself to. But it is the

16. See, e.g., Hans Morgenthau's general critique of the intellectual basis of the liberal tradition in *Scientific Man versus Power Politics* (Chicago: University of Chicago Press, 1946).

"adjusted" individual, the stereotyped individual, the individual who has forgotten how to be an individual, that pragmatism celebrates. Pragmatism is, indeed, the philosophy of our society—a society whose cult is to forget all unpleasantnesses and therewith most realities, a society in which "till death do us part" becomes "as long as we live" and the big bad wolf refrains with incredible decency from eating up the little pigs.

By comparison with this philosophy of glamour, Kierkegaard's writing, in all its narrowness and with all its drawn-out introspective agonizing, possesses, nevertheless, an intensity of emotion that impresses one with its power and that both frightens and illuminates by the insights that it now and then displays; for Kierkegaard does try to face the puzzle of the human individual, sometimes, indeed, in hackneyed and tedious contrasts between time and eternity, infinite and finite, but often in a character sketch or parable that sharply stresses some aspect of the general problem that forms the main preoccupation of existential philosophy—the theme of the contingency of human life, *Geworfenheit*, as Heidegger calls it. Death is the most dramatic, perhaps the ultimately determining, example of such contingency, and the dread of death the most dramatic, perhaps even the ultimately determining, attitude impelling human actions. But, more generally, what Kierkegaard and existentialism are concerned with is the stubbornness of fact not as data to be understood but as the necessity for free beings to be just this and not that; the impingement of the sheer brute givenness of each person's history on his aspirations as an individual; the desperate conflict in the individual's nature established by such impingement; the extreme isolation and incommunicability of that conflict in its sheer immediate qualitative character. Conrad's Lord Jim, for example, seems to me in this sense an existential character, staking his whole life, as he does, on the refutation of a single past action. And in this connection the devious "indirect communication" of Conrad's novels bears a significant likeness to Kierkegaard's kind of literary technique. The tragic conflict that lies at the core of personal existence is something completely private, completely hidden at most times from public view, and revealed only in glimpses as the story-teller develops his tale. The maximum of conflict, the maximum of isolation, are what Conrad, like existentialism, stresses in the experience of the individual person. A better example, for that matter, because it comes from the current existential school itself, is the character of Garcin in Sartre's *Huis-clos*, who has not just his life but all eternity to puzzle out the question of his cowardice. Or take an example in Kierkegaard himself: his favorite Old Testament theme of the sacrifice of Isaac. This, though a very different situation, is marked by the same agony of inner conflict. Here is Abraham, lifting the knife to slay Isaac whom he loves; the moment is inescapable, yet its necessity is at once divine will and sore temptation. Or, again, a favorite character with Kierkegaard is the ironic individual, in whom appearance and reality are at the extremest odds with each other. The novel emphasis in existential philosophy, in short, is its attention everywhere to the meaninglessness that continually underlies significance in human life—a substratum of nothingness as clearly exhibited in contingency as such as in death, the ultimate contingent.

There is in this kind of conception, bizarre and limited though it seems, a dynamic really novel in Western thought; and this dynamic Kierkegaard does genuinely contribute as a fresh source of philosophizing, implying not merely a reorganization of philosophic categories but a renewal of philosophic vision.

6

But what of the philosophic implementation of Kierkegaard's thought? He calls himself a "dialectical poet": "I am a poet, but of a peculiar kind, for the dialectical is the natural determination of my essence."[17] What, then, has Kierkegaard the dialectician to offer, technically, for those queer souls who have to express their perspective on human experience not in poetry or painting but in abstract categories and logical inferences? A little, I think, though not much.

For one thing, in Kierkegaard's analysis of the modalities there is a rather interesting construction of modal spheres. The merely possible equated to the necessary is contrasted with the actual equated to the contingent; the necessary as the logically possible to the nonnecessary, actually possible; the actually possible to the actually real; and so on. This construction is used partly in the analysis of logic as the sphere of the merely possible by which Kierkegaard refutes the Hegelian conception of a logic equivalent to ontology; partly in the analysis of freedom as the nonnecessary and of subjectivity as the actual, therefore more than merely possible, therefore nonlogical, and, directly at least, incommunicable. On some special points in this general context—for example, the conception of the past as equally nonnecessary with the future and of the historian as a "backward prophet"—there are some provocative, if not entirely plausible, passages. In general, however, Kierkegaard's analysis of the modalities is not strikingly original. He drew a good deal from the modified Aristotelianism of Trendelenburg, whom he evidently studied closely; and, though he disagrees explicitly with the Aristotelian division of possibles, his general analysis does not diverge markedly from the position of all those philosophers who have taken pains to separate the knowledge of logic or propositions or inference from the knowledge of things.

The existential dialectic itself, secondly, involves at least one central conception that is of great significance for contemporary existentialism—the concept of the "leap." The

17. *P*, IX, A, 213.

dialectic as a whole in Kierkegaard has its chief significance in the peculiar religious stage into which it issues. The first, aesthetic stage (the life of the sensuous moment) has meaning only in its collapse before the reality of time. Face to face with the temporality of his own existence, the individual tries, in the ethical phase, to turn temporal flux into true history by reference to an absolute moral standard. But duty cannot in Kierkegaard come even as close as it does in Kant to standing by itself. The whole significance of this second stage, again, lies in its collapse, in the realization that all duties are toward God—hence, for example, Abraham's duty to slay Isaac, an action which may look like the very opposite of morality humanly seen, since morality cannot be humanly seen at all. So the whole movement has its whole meaning in the emergence of the third, religious stage, in which the individual, totally isolated from his follow-men, stands in the shattering realization of his own unworthiness before his God. In this singly directed movement it is the final stage rather than the technical manipulation of the process that is significant. But what is peculiar and important along the course of the dialectic is the stress on the discontinuity of personal existence that Kierkegaard everywhere displays. From the aesthetic to the ethical, as from the ethical to the religious, phase, the transition is by a leap. Even in the knowing process (see Kierkegaard on Heiberg, p. 18) and a fortiori in the sphere of morality and religion, every significant step implies an absolute disjunction, a radical shift of categories, like that on which Kierkegaard likes to dwell from quantity to quality. It would be interesting to compare Kierkegaard's thought here with Bergson's analysis of subjective experience. They share the notion that the immediate temporal flux of our experience is the sphere of quality, which is misunderstood by the quantifying abstractions of the intellect. But Bergson identifies the subjective with the continuous, the snowball that swells as it advances. For Kierkegaard, on the other hand, continuity is the mark of the logical and unreal; and the actual inner growth of the person is characterized by radical discontinuity at every important stage.

7

With these exceptions, however, Kierkegaard judged as philosopher rather than as inspiration to philosophers cuts an extremely poor figure. Pacing his eight rooms at Kongens-Nytorv, each of them equipped with a standing-height desk, Kierkegaard thought and thought and wrote and wrote. In the papers certainly every passing thought was caressingly noted, drawn out, repeated again and again; and too much of such verbiage found its way into the works themselves. After all, there was no one to stop him. He was not checked by his friends, for his only "friends" were the superficial acquaintance of the coffee-house, who presumably remained, to use his language, at the aesthetic stage of existence. He was not restrained by publishers, for he lived on his capital—which conveniently survived as long as he did—and depended financially on no one. He was not affected by popular acclaim or the reverse, since he hated the crowd as cordially as a "subjective thinker" was bound to do. I do not mean to suggest that no philosopher can write without contact or criticism from outside; there have been philosophers, like Eriugena, for example, who seem to have risen singly to greatness out of the most barren environment. But, if it can be done, Kierkegaard was not the man to do it. The worst is not even the repetitious *apologiae pro vita sua*, dealing with what Kierkegaard admits to be bagatelles for the outside, though tremendous problems to himself—the problem of the pseudonyms, for instance; the problem of his relation to Regina, rehashed years after the break with her; and so on. Besides all these, one finds in the works and papers, interspersed between brilliant insights and moving parables, page after page of childishly bad logic—and, what is worse in a critic of the "System," bad Hegelian logic; of pure word-juggling and of paradoxes, nicely pointed, indeed, but meaningless or more frequently simply untrue. A few examples will suffice here; they can be multiplied endlessly throughout the nearly thirty volumes of works and papers.

In the *Philosophical Fragments* Kierkegaard is dealing with the question of how, from historical knowledge, one can attain eternal blessedness. He starts with the Socratic problem: How can one learn if one does not in some sense already know what one has to learn? The Socratic solution (recollection) does not, Kierkegaard says, emphasize the *moment* of decision; he is looking for an account which does. But if the moment is to be decisive,

then until the moment the seeker must not have had the truth, not even in the form of ignorance, for then the moment becomes merely the moment of stimulation. In fact he must not even be the seeker; for it is thus that we must express the difficulty if we do not want to explain it socratically. So he must be determined as outside the truth (not coming to it, as proselyte, but coming from it) or as untruth. He is untruth. But how shall one remind him, or what help will it be to remind him of what he has never known and so cannot think of?[18]

What does it mean to say the seeker *is untruth?* What Kierkegaard wants, of course, is the simplest form of contrast between man, who "is falsity," and God, who is truth: "The teacher is God himself, who acting as occasion gives occasion to the learner's being reminded that he is untruth, and by his own fault. But this condition, to be untruth and to be it by one's own fault, what can we call it? Let us call it *sin*."[19] Quite apart from the theological question of defining sin on this purely intellectual basis, the inference itself, from the ignorance of the individual to the statement, "He is untruth," seems the simplest sort of non sequitur.

Or consider this passage: "In so far as the learner is in

18. *S*, IV, 207.   19. *Ibid.*, IV, 209.

untruth, but is so with himself . . . . it might seem that he was free; for to be with one's self [hos sig selv] is, in fact, freedom."[20] Here is the Hegelian definition (das bei sich selbst Sein), patly taken as part of the argument, though the whole superstructure of Hegelian thought which could make it anything but nonsense has been roundly rejected. To be sure, it turns out that the learner is not free—God must free him—but the Hegelian definition is nevertheless used as the starting-point for that discovery; it is not the definition, but the fact, that is denied.

And along with Hegelian definitions, Kierkegaard retains the Hegelian habit of paradoxical play with philosophical vocabulary. In criticism of the definition of necessity as unity of possibility and actuality, for example, he says: "What could that mean? Possibility and actuality are not different in essence, but in being; how could there, of this difference, be formed a unity which was necessity, which is not a determination of being but of essence, since the essence of the necessary is to be."[21] That seems to me at least as crude as the play on Wesen/gewesen that Kierkegaard himself derides. Or, in dealing with the question of the contemporaneity of those who saw and spoke with God on earth, he says:

But what does that mean, that one can be contemporary without being contemporary, and thus one can be contemporary and yet, despite using this advantage (in the immediate sense), be the noncontemporary; what does that mean except that one simply cannot be immediately contemporary with such a teacher or circumstance, so that the real contemporary is not the real contemporary in virtue of immediate contemporaneity, but in virtue of something else? So: the contemporary can, despite that, be the noncontemporary; the real contemporary is so not in virtue of immediate contemporaneity, therefore likewise the noncontemporary (in the immediate sense) can be the contemporary through the other consideration by which the contemporary becomes the

20. Ibid.   21. Ibid., IV, 266.

[34]

real contemporary. But the noncontemporary (in the immediate sense) is, in fact, the later, so the later may be the real contemporary.[22]

Why all this word-play when the next sentence makes the same point so much more tellingly?

Or is it this to be the contemporary, and is this the contemporary we honor, who can say: "I ate and drank before his eyes, and that teacher taught in our streets; I saw him many times; he was an insignificant man of low birth, and only some few believed they found anything extraordinary in him, which I could not in the least discover, even though when it comes to being contemporary with him, I was that, in despite of any one"? Or is it this to be contemporary, and is this the contemporary, to whom God may say if they meet sometime in another life and he wants to appeal to his contemporaneity: "I know you not"?[23]

The trouble is, Kierkegaard never did reject his Hegelian background. He got some genuine insight into its narrowness from his teachers Møller and Sibbern, and he brought to bear on a certain type of dialectical philosophy a genuine passion of his own that now and then has philosophical implications. But he remained, in the main, within the intellectual horizon of the secondhand Hegelianism that his own epigram so aptly describes: "What the philosophers say about reality is often just as disappointing as it is when you read on a sign at a second-hand store: 'Ironing done here.' If you should come with your clothes to get them ironed, you'd be fooled; for only the sign is for sale."[24] Within that limited horizon, moreover, the source both of the weakness and the strength of Kierkegaard's philosophy is his love of paradox. Paradoxes are sometimes true and sometimes false, but he cherished them for their own sake. Granted that the paradox of the God-man did really hold deep meaning for him; that is clear from the power of the *Fragments*, where the question is explicitly focused from the start on that par-

22. *Ibid.*, IV, 259.
23. *Ibid.*, IV, 259–60.   24. *Ibid.*, I, 19.

ticular "absolute" paradox, as against the more discursive *Postscript*, where the movement is from the analysis of the modalities to paradox as such. Granted, too, that the necessity for paradox in the indirect communication of the subjective is genuinely a consequence of Kierkegaard's interpretation of conceptual knowledge. But much of Kierkegaard's writing seems to be motivated not so much by an insight into the philosophical or religious appropriateness of paradox to a peculiar problem as by the sheer intellectual delight in the absurd for its own sake. Kierkegaard admitted his own inclination to "deceive himself with language"; and one suspects that in his perpetual coining of paradoxes such deception often plays a rather heavy role. Consider the "schema for the exclusion or absence of inwardness" in *The Concept of Dread:* "Every form of the exclusion of inwardness is either activity-passivity, or passivity-activity, and whether it is the one or the other lies in self-reflection."[25] One of the examples of the schema is the following:

Pride—cowardice: Pride begins through an activity, cowardice through a passivity, otherwise they are identical; for there is in cowardice just so much activity, that the dread of good can be preserved. Pride is a profound cowardice; for it is cowardly enough not to want to understand what the proud in truth is; as soon as this understanding is forced on it, it is cowardly, blows up like a bomb, and bursts like a bubble. Cowardice is a profound pride, for it is cowardly enough not to want to understand even the demands of misunderstood pride; but by such reluctance it shows its very pride, and it knows, too, how to take into account that it has suffered no defeat and is therefore proud of the negative expression of pride, that it has never suffered any loss. It has also happened in life that a very proud individual was cowardly enough never to dare anything, cowardly enough to be as little as possible, just to save his pride. If one put together an active-proud and a passive-proud individual, one would have an opportunity, in the very moment when the first collapsed, to persuade one's self how proud at bottom the coward was.[26]

25. *Ibid.*, IV, 451. 26. *Ibid.*, IV, 455.

This is a startling passage; but does it startle because of an unusual insight or simply because it involves some rapid conjuring tricks with an unusual pair of contraries?

Or consider Kierkegaard's statement of the question before us: the place of paradox in thought:

Paradox is the passion of thought; and the thinker who is without paradox is like a lover without passion—an inconsiderable fellow. But the highest power of every passion is always to want its own destruction, and so it is likewise the highest passion of the understanding to want a stumbling block, even though the stumbling block may in one way or another prove its destruction. That is thought's highest paradox, to want to discover something it cannot think.[27]

Again, this is a rather intriguing passage; but is it true that every passion seeks its own destruction? Yet it is on that at least doubtful proposition that the argument hinges. If a thinker without paradox is an inconsiderable fellow, the thinker who loves the absurd for its own sake is, in his own way, a questionable character, for he may easily turn out as much falsity as truth or as much nonsense as sense.

8

But Kierkegaard's greatest weakness is not even his shabby Hegelianism or his overindulgence in verbal sleight of hand. It is the inadequacy of the man himself to bring to fruition the redirection of philosophy that he initiates.

The significance of the existential dialectic lies, as I have said, in the final religious stage that alone gives meaning to the whole. The aesthetic is trivial, the ethical merely transitory; only in the religious stage does subjectivity come into its own. But what is this religious life that Kierkegaard exalts? It is the life of what he himself calls "an intensive point." Subjectivity can be truly subjective only in the confrontation of the individual with God, since only the absolute is com-

27. *Ibid.*, IV, 230.

pletely indescribable, completely beyond the inroads of abstraction and objectivity. Only before God is a man really himself, because it is only before God that he is finally and irretrievably alone. But before God the finite individual is as nothing; and it is the bitter realization of that nothingness that marks the religious stage of existence. Religious experience for Kierkegaard, in other words, lies wholly in the self's awareness of its infinite distance from the God whom alone it loves. And the quality of that awareness, the way it feels to the self, is pure and unmixed suffering. Sometimes, to be sure, the religious life is described as a joyous one: "over 70,000 fathoms, miles and miles from all human help, to be glad." But the quality of suffering is much more frequently what Kierkegaard stresses in the "intensive" existence he has chosen. To persist in the direction of intensiveness, he says, is "nothing more nor less than to be sacrificed"; and the sheer unmitigated agony of spirit that accompanies the sacrifice is the triumphant issue of his dialectic of personal existence—for the intellect, pure paradox; for the spirit, pure suffering. This is indeed the life of the intensive point, "zero-point existence" (*Nullpunktsexistenz*) as some of its critics have called it. Granted that the march of the *Weltgeist* is indifferent to the salvation of one's single self; perhaps even that indifference is preferable to this sort of salvation.

The dialectic that leads to it is simple and straightforward—from outwardness to inwardness, that is, to complete, wholly isolated inwardness, with the only really private and incommunicable object, that is, the absolute, for content. But the absolute, which is infinite, cannot be content for the finite self. So there is nothing left but the tortured recognition of that inability to fill out the whole of subjective experience.

The question is whether turning to inwardness necessarily means turning to the self as totally isolated from other selves, and so turning completely away from any conception of human community; for in that case there is indeed nothing but the individual as nothing before God—or, when faith is gone, simply as nothing. Kierkegaard's preference for extremely simple disjunctions and, more especially, his own antisocial temper made him think that inference a compelling one: either the objective or the subjective; there is no compromise. True, he is so far right, that the root of morality does lie in the individual. That is, in fact, one of the significant insights that existential philosophy has to offer as against current social-work, social-conscience gospels. It is, indeed, meaningless to find moral value in helping others if one does so out of despair at finding such value in one's self. If human individuals as such, those helping as well as those helped, are not thought of as possessing by their very humanity some core of intrinsic worth, the end of helping them represents only an endless process of running away from one's own emptiness. Kant's principle, "Treat every human being as an end and never as a means," holds only if one's own self is equally an end with every other. But to focus only on one's self in total isolation is to take an equally distorted, if not an impossible, view of human nature—and Kierkegaard's description of the ethical stage is, in fact, highly artificial and unconvincing; for morality is equally meaningless without some conception of a community in which the individual is set. Yet Kierkegaard rejects philosophically and personally any such notion: community means outwardness, a denial of self, and therewith falsity, hypocrisy, self-deceit. And he rejects it, I think, out of weakness rather than out of strength. He could not, as he says, "realize the general"; and this inability stands behind his bitterness against all that is not in the extremest sense inward and subjective. The community that he himself appeared to live in was the highly artificial little world of Copenhagen café society, which suited him presumably just because he did not really live in it at all, because he could think his own thoughts in as near

[39]

to total isolation as a man can easily achieve. The irony of such a life is a little man's irony, different from the Socratic irony that Kierkegaard so much admired. From such a situation, to be sure, the philosophy of paradox and pain is a necessary consequence; but it is not a universal human situation, and the consequences to be drawn from it constitute, at best, but a twisted and fragmentary dialectic of personal existence.

Kierkegaard was a small man in a small society in a small intellectual world. He possessed genuine literary gifts of a limited sort, in particular, a genuine gift of parable—see, for example, the story of the lily and the bird or, in the *Fragments*, the story of the king and the lowly maiden. He was filled with genuine passion in the realization of an ethical and religious crisis, a passion which impels him at times to genuine philosophic insights. But that drive in him was limited as much by his spiritual stature as by the horizon of his intellectual vision. Kierkegaard, in other words, gave the Copernican revolution of philosophy still another turn, which it, in fact, needed; but he was himself too exclusively a shaper of paradox and, in the worst sense of that epithet, too "Hegelian" a thinker to give adequate philosophic implementation to such a new direction, and too small a man, for all his passionate self-torture, to make of the new dialectic more than the passage from aesthetic despair to a love of God equally despairing.

CHAPTER THREE

SARTRE AND HEIDEGGER: THE FREE RESOLVE

1

THE "stages on life's way," as Kierkegaard describes them, are, first and last, steps in a pilgrimage from the world to God; it is the ultimate confrontation of the individual with his maker that motivates and directs the journey. Only to find God could one relinquish the brightness of things seen for the dark despair of the mind turned in upon itself; only to find God could one renounce the splendid dream-palaces of speculative fancy for the cramped quarters of one's tortured solitary self. But, in the view of Sartre and, by Sartre's account, of Heidegger, it is the very denial of God's existence, not the search for him, that makes the inner odyssey of the self seeking the self philosophy's primary concern. The self that existentialism[1] seeks is each person's individual self, which he must forge for himself out of such senseless circumstances, such meaningless limitations, as are given him. This self-creation—the making of one's essence from mere existence—is demanded of each of us because, according to existentialism, there is no *single* essence of humanity to which we may logically turn as standard or model for making ourselves thus or so. And there is no single concept of humanity, because there is no God. For the concept of a human nature, Sartre believes, was a by-product of the traditional idea of God the maker; and so, when God dies, the

---

1. In referring to "existentialism" in this and the next two chapters, I am referring to contemporary atheistic existentialism, such as that of Sartre and Heidegger.

notion of an essence of humanity dies with him, leaving just these particular histories of these particular selves to "live themselves subjectively" as best they can. God is traditionally thought of as a kind of supermanufacturer, who turns out men much as Ford turns out motorcars. And there is no sense in talking of a V-8 or a model T or even a timeless and eternal pattern of machines or men without a maker to make, or at least conceive, them. A man, then, is either made by God in conformity with that "superior artisan's" superior model, or he must make himself out of the brute facts of his own particular situation without any model at all. According to Sartre, however, God is impossible. To be God is to exist from the necessity of his own nature alone: to be *causa sui*. But to be the cause of one's self is to stand in relation to one's self: that is, to be at a distance from one's self, to be what one is not, to be in the manner of consciousness, which is aware of *not* being its own foundation—that is, to be not necessary but contingent. Necessary existence, then, implies its own contradictory, contingent, or nonnecessary existence and is therefore impossible. In other words, if God existed, he would be contingent and hence not God; or if he is God, he is not contingent and hence, since noncontingent existence is self-contradictory, is not. But if we have no maker, neither is there a model by which we can trace the proper pattern of humanity, since the model was conceived of only as an instrument of the maker. "Heaven is empty," and we are left alone to create ourselves by our own acts.

This is perhaps a crude paraphrase of Sartre's argument; but the argument itself, on contingency and necessity, though stated with more complexity than I have given it, is not essentially different and is, in my opinion, a very questionable one. Actually, however, what is important for Sartre's position is not the disproof of God's existence but, much more simply, the absence of any belief in his existence. Granted, on whatever grounds, the logical impossibility of the traditional God: that is, for a Kierkegaard, just the reason to cherish our faith in him. Logical impossibility can no more conquer faith than logical possibility can create it. What matters, then, is not the inaccessibility of God to logic but the actual fact that we do not believe in him; for, as such different Christians as Augustine or Occam have recognized, if faith in an all-good, all-powerful maker of all things does not precede our reasoning, no argument will ever lead us to him. Therefore, if we start, as Sartre does, without that essential faith, we are indeed left with the naked facts of our contingent existences to make of what we may. There is no nature and, a fortiori, no human nature, ordered through and through by the plan of a supreme and supremely wise Creator, on which our acts and aspirations can be modeled and by which they can be judged.

There is, however, another possible position which one might oppose to that of the existentialist. Why, even without a creator, cannot the human species, qua natural species, have one uniform and intelligible essence? The analogy with human processes of manufacture—motorcar models for motorcar-makers—is a rather shaky one, especially in view of the fact that in Aristotle we have an actual historical instance of a philosophy involving a unitary human nature but not a creating God. The pure Aristotelian position, as against the Platonized and Judaized Aristotelianism of Christianity, Sartre does not anywhere, so far as I know, trouble to dispose of. He could have shown fairly easily, I should think, that it is, if not an untenable, at least a fairly unlikely, position in the face of a number of kinds of evidence. For instance, there is the familiar objection to Aristotle's eternally separate species in the light of the theory of organic evolution. This can be got around, perhaps, by devious logic; but, unless one starts with the notion of a world of God's creatures permanently ordered, there seems to be little ground for maintaining the Aristotelian species against the much weightier evidence for

[43]

some sort of continuum of living things. Not only biology, moreover, but modern physics as well lends its weight against the tightly ordered neatness of an Aristotelian universe. Nor is there in Aristotle's psychology any place for the complexities of the subconscious, which are, surely, neither aspects of the sensitive soul that we share with animals nor expressions of a rational and actively knowing faculty. In short, without the support of a supernatural faith or the excuse of a perverse antiquarianism, our concept of matter, life, or mind equally refuses to be bound by the fetters of Aristotelian procedure; and so we lose whatever advantage might have accrued to us morally from an acceptance of the notion of a neatly divided and subdivided nature, including one nicely unified and definable compartment labeled "Man." In fact, then, Sartre's position is not seriously weakened by his failure to deal with the Aristotelian essence of humanity. Yet it is still a strange omission on his part, since the existence of the Aristotelian system does clearly invalidate the simple inference, "No God, therefore no essence of man."

But, if divinely or philosophically given essences are eliminated, neither is human nature here reduced to material categories. Materialism is, I presume, beneath the ontological dignity of Heidegger even to refute; but the philosophy that reduces man to mechanism has, for Sartre at least, enough attractiveness to merit refutation. The political position of the French existentialists, as the article quoted in chapter i indicates and as we shall see in more detail in a later chapter, is definitely left of liberal. And just because they share political aims and sympathies with the Communists, they take special pains to show how, in their view, existentialism provides a better philosophic basis for these aims than does Marxist materialism. There is even a note of personal sympathy—an affect not generally conspicuous among them—in some of their dealings with communism. See, for example, in Sartre's *Age of Reason*, the interview of his admittedly autobiographical hero, Mathieu, with his Communist former friend. A sharp nostalgia and a kind of sympathetic envy dominate Mathieu's mood: he feels more bitterly than usual the loneliness of his search for freedom, which as clearly involves his condemnation by the revolutionary friend he more than halfway admires, as it does his rejection by the bourgeois brother he despises.

In Sartre's own philosophy, moreover, the concept of body, which, as he points out, is strangely ignored in Heidegger, is central to the analysis of consciousness; but it is *this* body and *these* factual conditions as a facet of *this* personality that are significant, not personality as such, reduced in general to an epiphenomenon of abstract material laws. To "explain" consciousness even as mechanically as analysis tends to do, by turning typical conscious symptoms into the expressions of universally recognizable subconscious patterns, is, for Sartre, to avoid the problem of the individual consciousness itself. True, Sartre takes a great deal from analysis in his transformation of symbol interpretation into "existential psychoanalysis"; but in the ultimate philosophical meaning and human purport of such interpretation there is a significant difference. In *L'Être et le néant*, after a detailed discussion of the symbolic meaning of *la viscosité* and *les trous*, he concludes:

.... What interests the [existential] psychoanalyst first of all, is to determine the free project of the single person starting from the individual relation which unites it to these different symbols of being. I can love viscous contacts; have a horror of holes, etc. That does not mean that the viscous, the greasy, the hole, etc., have lost their general ontological significance for me, but, on the contrary, that, because of that signification, I determine myself in such and such a manner in relation to them.[2]

What the existential psychoanalyst is after, it seems, is not so much the elimination of the problems of the conscious

2. Jean-Paul Sartre, *L'Être et le néant* (Paris: Librairie Gallimard, 1943), p. 706.

self through explanation of their origin in typical subconscious patterns as it is the use made of universal symbols by *this* individual—and that is a free use. The existentialist does not deny the reality of the individual will by uncovering the cause-and-effect relations that determine its choices and reducing it to them. Rather, he illuminates the individual will and heightens our sense of its reality by discovering how, with respect to the fundamental project that constitutes myself, *I determine myself* in relation to such symbols.

But if the ordinary analyst's determinism is inadequate from the existentialist point of view, at least as much so is the Marxist attempt to reduce consciousness to materially determined cause-and-effect phenomena. The economic determinants that make me worker, farmer, or entrepreneur, housewife, "career woman," or "socialite," have for the existentialist enormous and inescapable importance for the direction and purport of the history that is or becomes myself. There is, for existentialism, no free-will-in-itself existing inwardly, in Stoic fashion, in eternal apartness from the afflictions or achievements of the existing, embodied individual. There is no inner versus outer, rational versus irrational, in human histories. But, on the other hand, though there is no self *apart* from this particular economic, social, physical situation, such a situation does not *constitute* the self. No matter how bound by feudal oppression was the peasant whom Gibbon sneered at, there was a difference between him and the ox he worked. He could work well or ill, with docility or rebelliousness; he could even, on occasion, rise to rule Christendom; and he could sporadically, if ineffectively, exclaim with Wat Tyler, "When Adam delved and Eve span, who was then the gentleman?" Geographical, historical, and economic facts far beyond the individual's control do indeed determine the scope and the limits of the choices he can make. Yet, however narrow those limits, it is still the choice within the situation, not the mere situation itself, that makes the man. But materialism, as Sartre sees it, nullifies that central freedom; it makes us not only determined by things but ourselves things; and thus, in its revolutionary form, it involves the contradiction of seeking human liberty through its denial. At least it appears to seek it, though, at bottom, materialism is, for the existentialist, an endeavor not to find liberty but to avoid it, to seek excuses for rejecting a freedom one dare not face.

2

Existential philosophy, then—or that branch of it which Sartre calls "atheistic existentialism"—is an attempt to reinterpret human nature in terms of human subjectivity itself, not through superhuman religious or subhuman material categories. It is this attempt to show how human values are derived from a totally human—in fact, a desperately human —situation that makes some of the analyses of Sartre or Heidegger, if not valid, at least terribly relevant to the dilemma of those who can find comfort in no creed of God or science.

Before we look at some of the particulars of this reinterpretation, however, it should be noted parenthetically that to limit their philosophies to the sphere of human values and human problems would imply for either Sartre or Heidegger a very superficial and misleading conception of their aims; for both of them profess not to be dealing with "ethical" or even "epistemological" problems in the traditional sense but to be founding a new ontology, a new analysis of being itself, not our being as distinct from being in general. True, this new ontology is conspicuously focused on what look like human categories—in Heidegger, such concepts as concern, care, curiosity, dread of death, resolve, etc.; in Sartre, consciousness, interrogation, dread, bad faith, etc. Yet Heidegger is forever insisting on the distinction between the ontological significance of his principles and the merely

—and contemptibly—"ontic" application of them to particular actual situations. Sartre's *Being and Nothing*—as metaphysically entitled as its German parallel *Being and Time*—is explicitly said to be a work in ontology which merely lays the foundation for particular moral or psychological analysis of special human problems. Heidegger at the outset of *Sein und Zeit* declares he is embarking on a "destruction of ontology" as the preface to a new ontology. And Sartre claims to be analyzing the conscious self—the *pour-soi*—with the purpose of discovering, through its relation to things, the nature of phenomena as distinct from self, of what in Hegelian language he calls the *en-soi*. Yet, where "being" enters both investigations, it enters totally within the explicit context of its human bearing and personal significance; and to call this "ontology" seems, to one not trained in the discipline of Husserl and his school, a strange extension—or limitation—of the name. We all live, as Heidegger puts it, "under Kant's shadow." We all recognize, in some form, a distinction between what is and what appears to us; and in the light of that distinction we recognize that when we try to deal with being we must, from our limited perspective, deal with it not simply as it is but as it seems to us. But what Sartre and Heidegger profess is the exact contrary of that Kantian restriction: that in dealing with things as they *seem* to us we *are* dealing with them as they are. Here, I must humbly confess, I simply cannot follow them, unless in the spirit in which one follows Alice down the rabbit-hole. In its human relevance the analysis of both philosophers is genuinely novel and, in part at least, genuinely illuminating. But as ontology I cannot profess, and do not propose, to expound it.

Admittedly neglecting, then, the aims and achievements of existentialism as a metaphysical revolution, let us look at some of the basic conceptions of Sartre and Heidegger as they bear, frankly, on the problems of human personality—

not on reality as such but on man's reality. It is, after all, from its stress on human existence, not just existence, that the movement takes its name; and it is that stress, in its new concreteness, that gives it its importance, whether as momentary fashion simply—"le nouveau Da-da," as Sartre has called himself—or as something much more serious.

Looking at their work, then, in this limited context, one finds, equally in Sartre and in Heidegger, a number of fundamental concepts that appear, as in Kierkegaard, either new or newly interpreted when compared with more conventional theories of human nature. So, for example, the concept of freedom receives new meaning when it is seen in the context of the concrete human situation—neither as God's inexplicable gift to his image nor as the self-delusion of a cluster of conditioned reflexes. The net of circumstances that constitutes in the broadest sense my physical situation, the world into which I am flung—or rather into which, when I come to any kind of awareness, I have always already been flung—is, nevertheless, a world only through my projection of what I mean to make it. And some resolution to make of it one thing or another, to make of myself one person or another, is inescapable for me. Sheer facts exist only for "scum, offal, or a cabbage." For me they are always my facts, which I must transcend in some direction, if only in the direction of flight, of madness, or of self-destruction. There are steel and stones and mortar; but there is my city, which I must hate or love or be indifferent to, live in or leave or come back to. There are papers and typewriters and mailboxes; but there is my job, which I must get done by an editorial deadline or leave undone, with the sense (perhaps in either case) that existentialism is too much for me. Circumstances become circumstances only for the consciousness that tries to make of them something other than mere circumstances. So self and the world are continuously born together, in the self's free transcendence of its situation to form itself-in-

[49]

relation-to-its-world—a transcendence always already in process, yet always not yet accomplished. Thus it is no contradiction for men to be determined *and* free; for freedom would be meaningless, were there not these particulars to face or flee, use or discard—particulars which make me what I am, yet which I, by my transcendence of them in this direction and not in that, make into the world they are. So it is that "man is what he makes himself," that there is no essence of humanity but only actions of men—responsible acts, yet acts which are not yet what they aim to be.

Nor is this, as it may at first sight appear to be, just another easy way out of the problem of freedom and necessity. It is, on the contrary, an acutely uncomfortable way; for it implies not only hope of what I shall do, but literal and inescapable responsibility for what I have done. It implies not only that I may become what I may do, but that I am what I have done: not what, out of well-meaning incapacity, I meant but failed to do, but what, within the close yet flexible bounds of my personal situation, I *have* contrived to accomplish. Of such accomplishment and failure to accomplish I and I alone must bear the credit, the shame, the triumph, and the regret. It is meaningless to say with the materialist that my environment has made me what I am; for it is I who have, by the values I read into it, made it an environment. If malnutrition and bad housing made me a criminal, so have malnutrition and bad housing made poets, financial wizards, and what not. But if, contrary to the environmentalists' claim, I, not my situation, am responsible for what I am, such responsibility is not to be weakened by the conversion of myself into a secret, inner will, conveniently apart from my concrete, external, observable acts. There are, for the existentialists, no mute inglorious Miltons—if they are mute, they are *not* Miltons. There is no good saying I am what, but for my situation, I might have done; for if my situation *is* not myself, neither am I anything apart from it.

What I wish I might have been, had things been different, is an expression of my failure, not of my possible accomplishment. So there is, for the existentialist, a double compulsion of fact. There are the facts of my situation, meaningless except as I have given them meaning, and there are the facts of the meanings I *have* given and the acts in which I have expressed them: they were free acts, but, just because of that freedom, they are more intimately, more poignantly compulsive than the vast nexus of factors in my situation that are less immediately mine. Thus, shorn of materialist excuses or idealist escapes, the existentialist's judgment of men is ruthless and unforgiving in the extreme. It is, one may say, the exact opposite of Zossima or Dimitri's consciousness that we are all equally guilty. Each man is guilty alone and of himself: let him live out his own consequent hell without mercy and without reprieve. That is, in fact, what the characters of *Huis-clos* have to do—each serving only as goad or devil to the others. It is just the fact of his own action—which *was* cowardly—that Garcin cannot bear to face; as in the other example we mentioned earlier, it is the fact of his own action that *was* dishonorable that Conrad's Lord Jim is forever trying to escape. The hell of Garcin, the purgatory of Lord Jim, are the inevitable, right, and just consequences of human responsibility. Through some such hell, or at the least some such purgatory, each of us who is honest must dare to pass.

This is, one may say, a terrible doctrine. And, in fact, the realization of my responsibility to make of my world what it, and with it I, can be brings inescapably, when it is genuine, terror before the full meaning of that responsibility. Dread, though variously interpreted in Kierkegaard, Sartre, and Heidegger, invariably goes hand in hand with freedom. For all of them freedom is revealed not in heaven-written sanctions, not even in the smug humility of Kantian "respect for the law"—in which the law I give myself appears, despite its self-imposition, to follow universally from the nature of reason itself, and so to be comfortingly self-explanatory and self-justified. Freedom reveals itself rather, when we screw up our courage to see it without pretense, in the dizzying collapse of external sanctions and universal laws, in the appalling consciousness that I, and I alone, have, absurdly and without reason, brought order out of chaos; that I alone, crudely and stupidly, without cosmic meaning or rational ground, have made a world out of nothing: and with that awareness my world itself totters on the brink of the nothingness from which it came.

Strictly speaking, however, "terror" is not the word to describe this revelation of the meaning of freedom. Terror, like fear, has a definite object: the thing or the occasion that inspires terror or fear is a recognizable object or event *within* an ordered world—even if Sartre is right in describing the responding emotion as a "transformation of the world" aimed at eliminating the fear-inspiring object. The existentialists' "dread," by contrast—the vertigo that accompanies and even constitutes self-realization—has no definable object within a well-compartmentalized universe. It is a more ambiguous, even though a profounder, uneasiness, whose object is not this or that within our world but in some sense the very limits of that world itself. It is dread before emptiness—before annihilation—before nothing. Much scorn has been heaped on Heidegger, notably in Carnap's famous *Pseudoproblems of Metaphysics*, for his ontological effusions about nothing in *Was ist Metaphysik?* More recently Jean Wahl has criticized Sartre's arguments on nothing in *L'Être et le néant*. And there is certainly a good deal of word-play on the subject in both authors. "I am my own nothingness" (*Je suis mon propre néant*) is perhaps not quite so obviously nonsense as "Nothing nothings" (*Das Nichts nichtet*). But *le néant* like *das Nichts* does often provide a neatly dramatic phrase that seems to settle the author's problem with a quip rather than with an argument. Yet, with all that, the concept of dread with its object that is nothing and nowhere, the idea of human freedom as revealing itself in the very realization of its own meaninglessness, its own nonentity—such a conception lies at the core of existential philosophy and at the core of its significant contribution to man's view of his own nature.

That this dread is of nothingness is especially clear, perhaps, in Heidegger's analysis of personal existence; for in his view what is dreadful is the awareness of my death as the inevitable end toward which my freedom projects itself. Death in its utter negation of meaning limits, and so in the deepest sense determines, whatever resolve I make to turn the ineradicable past into a significant future. Yet it is only in such a resolve as limited by death—in the realization of my existence as essentially and necessarily *being to death*—that I can rise out of the distracting and deceiving cares of my day-by-day existence to become authentically myself. Only in such recognition of my radical finitude, in the sinking dread with which I face my own annihilation, can I escape the snares of a delusive present, to create, in a free resolve, a genuine future from a genuinely historical past.

For Sartre, on the other hand, my death is for me so complete a nonreality as to be of relatively little interest existentially. In the title-story of *Le Mur*, for example, the condemned man faced with death at sunrise becomes no longer a person but a mere mass of physical sensations. Existence with so hideously definite a limit to its future is no longer in any personal sense existence at all; for it is essentially the projection of myself into the future that constitutes, for Sartre, my personal reality. My own death, he says in *L'Être et le néant*, is more real for others than it is for me. Yet dread for him, too, is of a kind of nothingness. For Sartre it is the free resolve itself that is dreadful, since it carries with it the awareness that, unjustifiably and absurdly but inevitably, I must of my own single self create—or have created—the values that make my world a world. Hence the nothingness in the face of which dread rises is, though not death, just as genuinely a kind of annihilation or negation; it is the utter disparity between the bare facts that are there and the something else that is not, but which, without the comfort of divine sanction or material necessity, I in my agonized liberty must fashion of them. "Man is condemned to be free," that is, continually to make himself other than he is, and deep dread accompanies the awareness of that destiny.

But, one may object, our lives go on from day to day, through hopes and fears, rejoicings and disappointments, without any such sickening experience of the emptiness on which, the existentialists would have it, those lives are based. To the existentialist, however, that is no serious objection. If the actual experience of dread, the nausea in which it finds its physical expression, occurs but seldom, the very rarity of its occurrence testifies to its hidden presence; for it is characteristic of human freedom that it cannot bear, from day to day, to face the shattering awareness of its own reality. Hence dread, whether interpreted as in Heidegger as dread of death or as in Sartre as dread of liberty itself, is contrasted by both of them to an everyday self-deceiving manner of existence, which conceals the tragic terror of the individual's loneliness beneath a soothing multiplicity of conventional and external demands. Heidegger's "human existence" (*Dasein*) in continually lost in the "one": what one does, thinks, and becomes is substituted for the genuine resolve of the isolated but liberated individual. And such surrender to the scattered and distracting demands of every day is, though fraudulent, an essential aspect of the very existence of the individual. Being what we are, we cannot help living most of our lives, quantitatively speaking, in the little concerns of every day: in taking care of the things we habitually take care of[3]—the

3. The key concepts are *Sorge,* "care" or "concern," and *besorgen,* "take care of," or "be concerned with or for."

letters to be written, the dishes to be washed, the car to be greased, the class to be taught, the cigarette to be smoked. And in Sartre, in addition to the force of such everyday distractions, we find the ethical anguish of the free man blurred by various forms of "bad faith," i.e., attempts to blur the dichotomy between my freedom and the mere contingency on which it is founded, and thus to escape the awareness of the true nature of that freedom. Notable among these, e.g., is "the spirit of seriousness" which we mentioned earlier— the pretense to one's self of finding values comfortably ensconced for us in things, instead of realizing our own unjustifiable invention of them as unjustifiably carriers of our freedom. Such a pretense, in fact, is constantly abetted by the pattern of our daily lives:

.... Ordinarily, my attitude with respect to values is eminently reassuring. The fact is, I am engaged in a world of values. The anguished apperception of values as sustained in being by my liberty is a posterior and mediated phenomenon..... Thus, in what we shall call the "world of the immediate," which presents itself to our nonreflective consciousness, we do not appear first to be thrown afterward into undertakings. But our being is immediately "in situation," that is, it arises in undertakings and knows itself first in so far as it is reflected in its undertakings. We discover ourselves, then, in a world peopled with exigencies, at the heart of projects "in the course of realization": I am writing, I am going to smoke, I have an appointment tonight with Pierre, I must not forget to answer Simon, I have no right to hide the truth any longer from Claude. All these small passive expectations of the real, all these trite and everyday values, draw their meaning, in fact, from a first projection of myself which is, as it were, my choice of myself in the world. But, to speak precisely, this projection of myself toward a first possibility, which brings it about that there are values, appeals, expectations, and, in general, a world, does not appear except beyond the world as the abstract and logical sense and significance of my undertakings. For the rest there are, concretely, alarm clocks, signboards, tax returns, policemen—so many barriers against dread. But as soon as the undertaking fails me, as soon as I am sent back to myself because I must await myself in the future, I suddenly find myself to be the one who gives its meaning to the alarm clock, who forbids himself, at the instance of a signboard, to walk on a flower-bed or a lawn, who lends its urgency to the chief's order, who decides on the interest of the book he is writing, who brings it about, finally, that values exist to determine his action by their exigencies. I emerge alone and in dread in the face of the unique and first project which constitutes my being; all the barriers, all the railings, collapse, annihilated by the consciousness of my liberty; I have not, nor can I have, recourse to any value against the fact that it is I who maintain values in being; nothing can assure me against myself; cut off from the world and my essence by the nothing that I am, I have to realize the meaning of the world and of my essence: I decide it, alone, unjustifiable, and without excuse.[4]

3

Freedom that is total, yet rooted in a determinate, historical situation; dread in the face of such freedom; and the concealment of dread in the comforting frauds of everyday existence—such is the nexus of ideas that make up the core of the existentialist's conception of human life. There is, perhaps, nothing really new in any single one of these ideas. Kierkegaard, as we have seen, thought of himself as a continuer, though with a significant difference, of the tradition of Socratic irony. Sartre finds, overlaid, to be sure, with the falsities of "dogmatism" and "Christianity," the seed of his conception of free will in the unhampered liberty of the Cartesian God, who is bound neither by truth nor by good but makes them both. Here is the recognition, says Sartre, that liberty is at one with creativity, that only pure freedom can make a world. Even Heidegger, despite his scorn for nearly all philosophers but Heidegger, claims, with the help, it is true, of some rather strange philology, that he finds in the early pre-Socratics—Anaximander and Parmenides—some genuine existential insight. But, in general, philosophers

4. Sartre, op. cit., pp. 76–77.

have fought out the problem of freedom in a much more abstract sphere and have thus contrived, with singular persistence, to overlook the individual existence in which alone freedom can have its being, to obscure rather than to illuminate the grandeur and the folly, the triumph and the terror, of men's liberty.

Yet no theory of human nature that has truth in it is wholly new; and one finds instances of the truths stressed by contemporary existentialists, if not so much in their philosophic predecessors, at least certainly in the less logic-bound interpretations of human life of the poet or the novelist. Thus, for example, Simone de Beauvoir sees in Stendhal's Julien Sorel the existential hero, who would, in Napoleonic liberty, rise above his world and transform it. And the end of Julien, too, is, I should think, existentially fitting, for it expresses his fatal responsibility for an action that appears, in proportion to his ambition, capricious and even trivial. Or, again, Camus finds in Dostoievsky the existential novelist par excellence. That is because, in extreme contrast to his own philosophy of absurdism, whose heroes are Don Giovanni, the conqueror, the actor—those who glory in the sheer irrational moment—he equates existentialism with its religious form, with the morality that has passed through the absurd not to freedom simply but to God. Camus is mistaken in that equation. But if an Alyosha is unthinkable to the admirer of Julien, there is, for example, in the world as Ivan's Grand Inquisitor sees it, a reflection of something like the existentialist's sense of the bitterness of human freedom, though the existentialist would stoically bear that bitterness rather than demand that men renounce it for a false and captive happiness.

It has been said, too, that *Hamlet* is an existential drama;[5]

5. Cf. an article on *"Hamlet: The Existential Madness,"* by Wylie Sypher (in *Nation*, June 22, 1946), in which, however, there is some confusion between the absurdism of Camus and the existentialism of Sartre. "Absurdity" is an existential concept but not to the exclusion of other factors in the human situation.

and, though that is perhaps as hazardous as to call *Hamlet*, say, a Freudian drama or, in Friedrich Schlegel's sense, a metaphysical drama, still there is, in some respects at least, justice in the epithet. For the existentialist, every man is born to set right a time out of joint; and every man's tragedy, like Hamlet's, lies in the disproportion of the circumstances to be righted and the action that he takes to right them. This is not the simple romantic disparity of thought and action but a more delicate and, at the same time, more desperate discord. It is not just the dreams of a man at odds with what he does, but it is his dreams enacted, his values self-created and self-realized, hopelessly disproportionate to the circumstances he is trying to control. The actions that Hamlet does not take are as much actions as those that he does put into practice. The check that repeatedly keeps him from swift and effective execution of his purpose is as much his doing as are the bold and impulsive deeds that he *does* do in the heat of a moment—vis-à-vis Polonius, the pirates, at Ophelia's grave, and, finally, against the King himself. Or, to put it the other way, as the check where he should act points the lack of proportion between action and situation, so does the element of chance and of caprice in the actions which he does execute. The elements of chance in the plot—in the meeting with the pirates and in the final catastrophe—are by no means, as they appeared to Dr. Johnson, flaws in the structure of the play. They are dramatic instances of the absurdity, the irrationality, that underlies our freedom. Our highest purposes fall miserably and ineptly short of their fulfilment; and, where they do issue into positive action, they are ensnared in a maze of chance, purposelessness, or, at best, cross-purposes.

Not only the disproportion of circumstance and action, moreover, but the disharmony of a genuine humanity and its conventional imitation may be called, in a sense, an "existential" element in *Hamlet*. Hamlet's antic disposition is not simply a device to find out the king (it is put to little use for that or any other observable external purpose). It is, as the edge of Hamlet's wit continually bears witness, the sign of a deep wound—a wound originating in the sense of his mother's corruption but reflected more broadly in the rejection of the whole outer surface of his world, the world in which a man can smile and smile and be a villain. So Rosencrantz and Guildenstern, who were once accepted as friends or at least companions in student revelry, are now despised for the frauds they are; and Polonius is fittingly made a fool of. For Hamlet, there is that within which passeth show; but show is all the world of a Polonius or of Laertes, his youthful counterpart. Hamlet's apparent madness, like Kierkegaard's irony, marks the final, irremediable split between the worldly wisdom that is appearance only and the tragic reality which we find when we face ourselves unmasked.

And Ophelia's real madness echoes the same theme. Grief for her father may be the immediate occasion; but that grief cannot be disentangled from her equally grievous bewilderment about Hamlet, and that again is sharpened by the falsity of her own position. She has been preached at by father and brother, shamelessly used as a tool by her father—only in madness can a real Ophelia break through the restraints of such a situation. Some awareness of the frauds she is asked to live by is apparent even early in the play, in her reply to Laertes:

> But, good my brother,
> Do not, as some ungracious pastors do,
> Show me the steep and thorny way to heaven,
> Whiles, like a puffed and reckless libertine,
> Himself the primrose path of dalliance treads,
> And recks not his own rede.

It is that awareness, intensified by the further actions of the play, that, as her songs indicate, terminates in madness and, again in an action that appears half-accidental and half-willed, in death.

But one can find "existential" motifs in stranger places than *Hamlet*. One might not expect any kinship with existentialism, for example, in a novelist writing so entirely in a realistic tradition—and with so little claim to being a "philosophical" novelist—as Dickens. Yet the intimate relation of dread to the genesis and maintenance of a scheme of values is an "existential" theme dramatically exemplified, for instance, in *Great Expectations*. Of course one might hold, and with some reason, that Dickens would be, for an existentialist, merely a horrible example of "mauvaise foi": of a man who took so seriously the values given him by his age that he could not "rise above it to transform it." The boy in the blacking-factory, who so bitterly resented the vulgarity and sordidness of his surroundings, might as an artist create in rebel or criminal corrosives against the society in which he had again won the place of gentleman. But the bitterness growing from that childhood wound is the correlate of unquestioning acceptance of his society's values, not of their rejection or transmutation.[6] And that kind of acceptance constitutes the "spirit of seriousness" which the existentialists so profoundly scorn. In particular, the resolution of the story in *Great Expectations*—even without the false Estella ending—would probably appear to the existentialist to be exceedingly wicked. Pip is no longer the London gentleman; but, though exiled to the East and to trade, he is still undeniably a gentleman. His rather condescending visits to Joe and Biddy and his namesake scarcely atone for that (for Pip and Dickens) comfortable but (for the existentialist) shameful fact. As far as I can see, the only possible cures for *mauvaise foi* for Sartre and his followers are to be an honest workingman or an honest existential philosopher. But Pip could

6. See Edmund Wilson, "The Two Scrooges," in *The Wound and the Bow* (Cambridge: Houghton Mifflin Co., 1941).

hardly have turned into either of these worthy characters, any more than Dickens could.

Yet despite this (existentially) lamentable lack on the part of Pip and his author, the story of Pip's dream and its collapse does reflect, in part at least, a favorite existential theme. Miss Havisham, with her creature Estella, sets going Pip's discontent with himself as a "common laboring boy" with coarse hands and heavy boots—and his dreams of himself as something very different, as endowed by Fortune with the role and bearing of a gentleman. But Magwich and the prison-ship, on the other hand, are both the literal reality underlying that Fortune when it does come and the symbol of a psychological reality. The escape on the marshes fills small Pip with terror; that childhood terror is re-echoed in the nameless dread that he feels at the meeting with the convicts on the coach, and it comes fully to the forefront of his consciousness in the return of Magwich—when the gentleman of his daydream is brought face to face with the hideous reality of the outcast who has "made" him. As Miss Havisham is the external stimulus for Pip's situation and Estella the symbol of the beauty and grace he longs for, so Magwich and the convicts are the recurrent symbols of the terrible reality underlying the fulfilment of his hopes and of the uneasiness that accompanies the foreknowledge of that reality. The two themes coalesce only with Magwich's return; but their compresence is suggested in the episode of Pip's visit to Miss Havisham on the occasion of Estella's coming home as a "finished" young lady. This is seemingly the perfection of his dream: he is a gentleman, and Estella is meant for him. Coarse, humble Joe is totally banished, with obviously false but effective excuses; and the gentleman, like the lady, appears to be "finished." But it was on that journey that the convict of the pound notes traveled beside Pip on the coach, and that Pip got down off the coach at the edge of town to avoid their hearing his name:

[61]

As to the convicts, they went their way with the coach, and I knew at what point they would be spirited off to the river. In my fancy, I saw the boat with its convict crew waiting for them at the slime-washed stairs—again heard the gruff "Give way, you!" like an order to dogs—again saw the wicked Noah's Ark lying out on the black water.

I could not have said what I was afraid of, for my fear was altogether undefined and vague, but there was great fear upon me. As I walked on to the hotel, I felt that a dread, much exceeding the mere apprehension of a painful or disagreeable recognition, made me tremble. I am confident that it took no distinctness of shape, and that it was the revival for a few minutes of the terror of childhood.

It was indeed such a revival, but it was also an anticipation of the terror of adulthood—the anguish that was later to mark the collapse of Pip's illusions, the recognition of the squalor, uncouthness, and depravity from which, in fact, the realization of his vision of Pip the gentleman had sprung.

4

If the insights of existentialism are not entirely novel, however, their philosophic formulation in large part is. Not that age-old philosophic problems are here suddenly solved; but at least some of them are more adequately stated or some phenomena of human life more adequately described.

For example, look briefly at the problem of taste, the clearest and perhaps the most fundamental part of the whole question of the nature and origin of values. Disjoined from a foundation in some sort of Neo-Platonic world harmony, beauty tends in recent philosophy to become merely the expression of the sort of capricious liking about which there is proverbially no disputing. Such preferences can be listed or catalogued, and one can arrive statistically at a sort of "theory of value" just as one might arrive statistically at a general catalogue of the hair and eye color of various sections of the population. None of it seems very important for telling us either what this or that man is or what men in general are. But existentialism, with its stress on the project by which the individual creates himself, can, within the tradition of relativism and without recourse to absolutes or Ideas of Beauty, at least describe the phenomena of taste in their integral relation to what the individual essentially is or is becoming. Sartre's discussion of physical taste, of which all taste is in some sense a complex sublimation or elaboration, is startling, in part even fantastic. But it indicates a fruitful direction, according to him, for "existential psychoanalysis," perhaps even for aesthetic theory in general:

Thus *tastes* do not remain irreducible givens. If one knows how to question them, they reveal the fundamental projects of the person. Even preferences in food have a meaning. One will realize that, if one reflects well on the fact that every taste presents itself not as an *absurd* datum that should be excused but as an evident value. If I like the taste of garlic, it seems irrational that others can fail to like it. To eat is, in effect, to appropriate to one's self by destruction, and it is, at the same time, to stuff one's self with a certain being. And that being is given as a synthesis of temperature, of density, and of taste in the strict sense. In a word, this synthesis signifies a *certain being;* and when we eat, we do not limit ourselves, by taste, to *knowing* certain qualities of that being; by tasting it, we appropriate it to ourselves. Taste is assimilation; the tooth reveals, by the very act of grinding, the density of the body that it is transforming into a food bolus. Thus the synthetic intuition of the food is in its assimilative destruction. It reveals to me the being with which I am going to make my flesh. Hence what I accept or reject with disgust is the very being of that existent, or, if you prefer, the totality of the food proposes to me a certain mode of being of the being which I accept or refuse. . . . . .
. . . . One understands that taste, from this fact, receives a complex architecture and a differentiated matter—which presents to us a peculiar type of being—that we can assimilate or reject with nausea, according to our original project. It is therefore not

at all a matter of indifference to like oysters or clams, snails or shrimps, provided that we know how to disentangle the existential significance of these foods. Generally speaking, there is no irreducible taste or inclination. They all represent a certain appropriative choice of being.[7]

Or again within the tradition of relativism—say, within the line of non-Platonic, non-Hegelian philosophers of the last two centuries—there have been plenty who have denounced religion as (with Hume) superstition and enthusiasm or (with Marx) the opiate of the masses. The existentialism that we have been discussing obviously shares this antireligious bias. Yet at the same time the human reality of genuine religious feeling is not, as it is by most antireligious philosophers, simply dismissed as nonsense by existentialist writers. One has only to look at that greatest of skeptical texts, Hume's *Dialogues on Natural Religion*, to see what is lacking in this sort of enlightened refutation of faith. The *Dialogues* are an undoubted masterpiece of philosophical logic—I should not hesitate to say the most magnificent piece of philosophic writing in English—but as dialogues they have a strange weakness. Philo is the only person in them who is real, the only one whose arguments obviously rest on genuine convictions.[8] Cleanthes is a mere front, the man who, with eminent respectability and not much logic, takes the polite and moderate position. He is neither unreligious in his professions—heaven forbid!—nor too religious for comfort and decency. But poor Demea—again Hume-Philo makes the logic, or illogic, of his position painfully clear; but as a living person he is a null, or rather he is a bad Calvinist preacher trying to turn philosopher, which comes to much the same thing. And, most of all, apart from his

7. Sartre, *op. cit.*, pp. 706–7.
8. I am following here Norman Kemp-Smith's interpretation of the *Dialogues* (see his edition [Oxford: Clarendon Press, 1935]), which appears to me entirely conclusive, both on internal and on external evidence.

necessary place in the superb logic of the *Dialogues,* he is the incarnation of Hume's failure to understand what a genuinely religious disposition could conceivably be or how faith could be rooted in anything but the blindest enthusiasm or grossest superstition. Such narrowness is to some extent corrected, it seems to me, in the concreter analysis of Sartre and Heidegger. At least some concepts traditionally associated with religious beliefs are undeniably significant for them, though, of course, in a very different context. So, for example, guilt and conscience are essential to the resolve of Heidegger's *Dasein:* it is conscience that *calls* existence from the "one" to the realization of itself; and guilt is the consequence of that call: "Der Gewissensruf hat den Charakter des *Anrufs* des Daseins auf sein eigenstes Selbstseinkönnen und das in der Weise des *Aufrufs* zum eigensten Schuldigsein."[9] Or in *L'Être et le néant* one finds, for instance, such an analysis as this of original sin:

Shame is the perception of the *original fall,* not of the fact that I may have committed this or that fault, but simply of the fact that I have "fallen" into the world, into the midst of things, and that I need the mediation of another to be what I am. Modesty and, in particular, the fear of being surprised in a state of nakedness are only a symbolic specification of original shame: the body here symbolizes our object-character without defense. To clothe one's self is to disguise one's object-character, to reclaim the right of seeing without being seen, that is, of being pure subject. That is why the biblical symbol of the fall, after original sin, is the fact that Adam and Eve "know that they are naked."[10]

In both analyses there is much in the technical jargon that is oversubtle or even absurd, as, for instance, the typically Heideggerian statement (as the climax to a tortuous inquiry

9. Martin Heidegger, *Sein und Zeit* (Halle: Max Niemeyer, 1931), p. 269. If one can render Heidegger's weird language: "The call of conscience has the character of calling existence to its properest capacity of being itself, and that in the manner of calling it up to its properest guiltiness."
10. P. 349.

about the nature of the voice of conscience): "Conscience *speaks* only and constantly in the mode of *silence*."[11] And, what is perhaps more important, no one could claim that either of these writers is, any more than Hume was, in any generally accepted meaning of the word a "religious" man. But there is certainly in both of them insight into the human meaning of conceptions usually thought of as religious, an insight conspicuously lacking in philosophies that found their rebellion against the supernatural on broader than human models, whether it be the atom or the organism. In *L'Être et le néant*, as a matter of fact, even God, though nonexistent, takes on a novel meaning. In the continual transcendence of our past, striving to be not only free but—what we never are or can be—the foundation of our own freedom, God, *causa sui*, is what we hopelessly but inevitably will ourselves to become:

All human reality is a passion, in that it projects its own loss to found being and with the same blow to constitute the In-itself that escapes contingency by being its own foundation, the *Ens causa sui* which religions call "God." Thus the passion of man is the inverse of that of Christ, for man loses himself as man that God may come to birth. But the idea of God is contradictory, and we lose ourselves in vain; man is a useless passion.[12]

11. Heidegger, *op. cit.*, p. 273.
12. Sartre, *op. cit.*, p. 708.

CHAPTER FOUR

SARTRE AND HEIDEGGER: THE
SELF AND OTHER SELVES

1

So far we have been dealing with the solitary adventure in freedom of the single person, responsible by himself for what he makes of himself. Kierkegaard's stress on inwardness remains, even though not faith but its denial now motivates the turn to the subjective. Of Heidegger or Sartre, then, as of Kierkegaard, one is bound to ask: How is it that the individual, fallen strangely into a strange world, is yet not entirely alone? On the face of it at least, my existence involves that of others: whether, like Heidegger, I recognize the neighboring farmer's field as not mine and so acknowledge his existence or whether, like Sartre, I discover the existence of others in the absence of Pierre, who is not at the Flore, or in the presence of the waiter, who is—or more generally in the anonymous crowd of passengers among whom I find myself traveling in the Métro. How does the projection of myself in my world involve such other liberties, whose reality I appear to acknowledge at least implicitly in every hour of my everyday existence?

Heidegger gave, I suppose, what some people would call an answer to that question in his Heidelberg address, "Die Rolle der Universität im Neuen Reich" in which the freedom of *Sein und Zeit* turns out, in something like Hegelian fashion, to mean subjection to that higher entity—Hitler's Germany. It seemed to me then, and it still does, a disgraceful sellout of whatever core of genuineness underlies the ontological trappings of *Sein und Zeit*; for it *is* the complete iso-

[67]

lation of the free man, terribly alone with his own mortality, yet splendidly arrogant in face of the common world of the undifferentiated "one," that is real in Heidegger's analysis of human existence. To see in the surrender to the Nazi state the fulfilment of that hard-won freedom is, despite such affinities, for instance, as the anti-intellectualism of both Heidegger and the Nazis, to give away in advance whatever validity Heidegger's portrayal of human nature has. True, one ought not to consider existential philosophy apart from the existential philosopher; for, if every vision of the world is made what it is by the nature of its maker, so much the more so for a philosophy which professes to find in personal existence the subject, method, and fruit of its speculation. Nevertheless, the person behind the existentialism of Heidegger is, I should guess, not so much the Nazi Heidegger—a character as easily sloughed off as on, it seems—as the Heidegger of the Black Forest ski-hut: more dramatically alone in his snowworld than Kierkegaard or Sartre at their café tables of Paris now or Copenhagen then, and at least as sneeringly contemptuous as they of the self-delusions of those less "free."[1]

Sein und Zeit deals first with existence in the mode of *Verfallenheit*, that is, with existence as it loses itself in the distracting concerns of everyday. So the relation with other existences occurs, too, on this level. One phase of being-in-the-world is being-with-others. As things are "at hand" for my handling of them, so other human existences are there, too, with their everyday cares abetting or interfering with my own. This *Mitdasein*—i.e., "existing-with"—is, as Sartre justly observes, a highly abstract and impersonal relation. Heidegger's continual insistence on the "ontological" char-

1. For discussions of Heidegger's politics, i.e., the extent and significance of his association with the Nazis, see a pair of interviews published in *Les Temps modernes*, Vol. I, No. 4 (January, 1946), and Karl Löwith's article on the political implications of Heidegger's philosophy, in the same periodical, Vol. II, No. 14 (November, 1946). Löwith's aim is to show that Heidegger's naziism did, in fact, follow from his philosophical principles.

acter of his analysis and his rejection of the "ontic," that is, of the particular happenings of particular lives, as irrelevant to his profounder theme, do carry with them an emphasis on generalities which seems almost to contradict his initial assertion that *Dasein* is "mine in particular" (*je meines*). But even were such *Mitdasein* considered in particular cases rather than in general, it would still be, in the sphere of everyday existence, the conventional and therefore the general relation, say, of pupil to teacher, laborer to foreman, husband to wife; for on the level of everyday distraction, where the deepest direction of my own becoming is hidden by subservience to the "one," my relation to another, however close superficially, is likewise engulfed in the universal anonymity.

What one wonders is this: What happens to the individual's relationships to others when he resolves to be, not a mass of conventions, but himself? In other words, what does Heidegger do with the question of our existing-together-with-others outside the conventional and unauthentic level of existence? The answer is clearly "Next to nothing." My freedom is mine, and the awareness of it bears no intruders, for it is "freedom to death"; and from my loneliness in face of death no one can save me; nor can I, if I would, save or even pity another.

Heidegger does mention briefly that *Fürsorge*—the relation that I enter into toward others in my fraudulent everyday aspect—has an equivalent in the sphere of genuine existence. But it is a strange equivalent. On the everyday level, *Fürsorge*, as distinct from my general togetherness *with* others, is my direct concern *for* them. It corresponds, for persons, to the care I give things—and one's everyday life consists generally of a combination of the two. Thus as a housewife I take care of pots and pans, floors and linens, but I also take care of my husband and children. Or as an office worker I am concerned with files and accounts, papers and typewriters, but also with employers and employees. This is all in the purely conventional, fraudulent mode of existence; and here, of course, neither I nor the others emerge as genuine individuals but only as pseudo-centers in a pattern whose whole meaning is the distraction of the individual from his true nature. One might then expect, at first glance, that, with the transformation of myself into a genuine existence, I should also apprehend as genuine at least a few of the others with whom I habitually deal, and that therewith my concern for them would become a concern for them as genuine, not merely distracted, centers of human history. But such is far from being the case. I care for others in a genuine, rather than a conventional, sense, according to Heidegger, in so far as I refer my care for them essentially and completely *to my own free projection of myself*. This is, in other words, the contrary morality to Kant's: the free man is he who treats other people always as means, never as ends. But such a relation is hardly in any meaningful sense a togetherness of human beings or a concern for them. Rather it is the debasement of others to mere tools by the rare man of character who has risen to the level of a richer, genuine existence, who has resolved in ruthless independence to fashion a life-toward-death, a freedom in finitude on his own pattern. A relation, on the other hand, of concrete togetherness, in which two human beings stand as free beings face to face— such a relation the single-minded arrogance of Heidegger cannot envisage and could not tolerate.

There is another context in which one would expect Heidegger to deal with the individual as his relation to others affects his genuine existence, that is, in his discussion of historicity. The passage from the spurious to the authentic level of existence involves the translation of the chief existential concepts into temporal terms. The recognition of my finitude is the recognition of my existence as temporal; and my being-already-in-a-world, my everyday distraction in the present, my transcendent resolution toward the future, are all seen as dimensions of existential time. In this context *history* becomes a central concept. But "history" suggests to most of us, I should think, something more than the process of an individual life. History in the substantive sense—that is, the history about which "histories" are written—is, surely, as generally understood, the transformation or evolution of a group of lives lived together in some sort of functional, as well as merely physical, contiguity. Heidegger does, in fact, deal briefly with the relation of the togetherness of individuals to history. In part, he merely glances again at the togetherness of our conventional, fraudulent existence; in part he does some punning on *Geschick* and *Geschichtlichkeit*.[2] But his main emphasis, for instance, in the lengthy discussion of the views of Dilthey and the Count von Yorck, is still on the general distinction between a human life as a history and the mere being-there of nonhuman things. Sometimes, to be sure, this distinction implies a concept of community which goes beyond the individual. For example, in the analysis of historical monuments the point is made that as things they are not "historical," they are only there; they are "past" only in the sense that the human world in which they functioned is past. And such a world was, of course, the world of a group, a "civilization," not just an individual or an unrelated aggregate of individuals. But there is no explicit account of my history as shared with that of others who form part of the same history—no attempt to analyze the existential significance, if there be any, of the conception of community or tradition or the like. Nothing is added that makes my world in any real sense ours or lessens in any essential way the grim isolation of the self-resolved-in-face-of-death.

To be sure, Sartre, in his criticism of Heidegger's *Mitdasein*, stresses the fact that, for Heidegger, togetherness is es-

2. The pun is untranslatable; the words mean "fate" and "historicity," respectively.

sential to the very nature of the personal existent. That is so, in a way, in so far as Heidegger is unrelenting in his emphasis on the "ontological" and essential nature of every characteristic that he attributes to personal existence. And, indeed, on the level of the unauthentic, togetherness *is* essential; for it is just a fraudulent togetherness, a sense of belonging with nothing genuine to belong to, that constitutes the "one" in and by which, on the unauthentic level, each of us lives. On the other hand, with his resolute emergence into authenticity, Heidegger's individual learns to subordinate to their due place the concerns of everyday—and with them the people as much as the things that he is concerned with in this unauthentic aspect of his existence. In his distraction he was bound to the many: to many things and people and to that anonymous many, the "one," in whom his actions and his passions were submerged. Now he is liberated from the many by binding himself to a true one, that is, to his own solitary projection of himself into the future, a future shaped by the fearful realization of his mortal destiny. Here no one can follow him; he creates a world and a history out of the very fact of their inevitable cessation—and in that world or that history, as there is room for only one catastrophe, so there is room for only one solitary soliloquizing actor. Others are stage properties, placed perhaps by chance, but manipulated as he will by this strange virtuoso, playing, without author or audience, as his own sense of tragic fitness may direct.

2

As distinct from Heidegger, Sartre, at any rate, recognizes the importance of the problem of the relation between individuals and has dealt with it explicitly in at least two places: in the essay *L'Existentialisme est-il un humanisme?*[3] a talk

3. Jean-Paul Sartre, *L'Existentialisme est-il un humanisme?* (Paris: Editions Nagel, 1946). This essay appeared in translation under the title *Existentialism* (New York: Philosophical Library, 1947).

to the Club Maintenant published in 1946 and, in great detail, in Part III of *L'Être et le néant* (1943). These two expositions differ so markedly that they had best be dealt with separately. I shall take the later, and weaker, one first. (Presumably, Sartre cannot in either version be taken as speaking for French existentialism in general, witness the rather different analysis of Simone de Beauvoir in *Cineas and Pyrrhus*.)

The essay is a defense of existentialism against its attackers, principally Catholics and Communists. As such it blurs any distinctions among atheistic existentialists themselves—differences of Sartre's own doctrines from Heidegger's, for instance, which are stressed in *L'Être et le néant*—and does a good deal of sugar-coating of existentialism in general, notably on this very question of intersubjective communication. Subjectivity, Sartre says here, means not the individual consciousness but human subjectivity in general: that is the "deep sense" in which existentialists use the term when they say men cannot in their interpretation of experience go beyond the limits of the subjective. Such implementation as Sartre gives this conception here, however, is slight and extremely slippery. Man, he says, is what he makes himself; but when a man chooses for himself, he chooses likewise for all, for he chooses what is good, and what is good for one is good for all. So if a worker joins a Christian trade-union, he chooses a certain type of society as preferable over others for his fellows as well for himself. That seems plausible. But Sartre goes on: when I decide to marry, raise a family, or the like, I am again deciding for all mankind. That begins to sound remarkably like Kant's abstract argument for marriage; and one stops to wonder how, apart from a human nature, what is good for one can in any sense be good for all —whether the Christian worker, too, does not rather choose out of the available associations the one that best suits *him*

[73]

and only very incidentally, if at all, the one that he feels would be good for everyone.

The examples which Sartre uses in explication of central existential concepts confirm one's suspicion that he is arguing, extremely cleverly but, in Plato's sense, sophistically, with the end of persuasion not of truth. Dread, he says here, is the result of the very fact that, in choosing, I choose for all. It is exactly the feeling of a general deciding to risk his army's lives in this advance or that retreat. But that is a transformation beyond all recognition of the existential concept of dread, whether Kierkegaard's or Heidegger's or that of Sartre himself. Garcin of *Huis-clos*, Oreste of *Les Mouches*, Mathieu of *L'Age de Raison*—none of them is concerned with the universal implications of his acts but only with the question of how those acts themselves are or become or have been free, and with the awful implications of that freedom—for himself. They all must, of course, act in social situations—Garcin in relation to his wife and mistress or in the broader social situation of his condemnation to death; Oreste in the return to his people, in the desire to be one of them but, at the same time, to transcend them as their conscience; even Mathieu in his relation to the conventional class pattern that he refuses, as well as in his particular dealings with his mistress, with Ivich, etc. Yet in the case of all these Sartrean heroes, it is ultimately not the social setting that matters, not the implication of their behavior for others, but the meaning of their acts for their own liberty: for Garcin, the gnawing question, *Did* he die a coward? for Oreste, the search for his own triumph in his own act; for Mathieu, the question, over and over, How can he act in and for freedom and freedom only? And it is the awareness of that freedom, which is each man's concern and his alone, that constitutes dread: "Dread is the reflective grasp of freedom by itself."[4] If dread means anything, it is the agony of that

4. Sartre, *L'Être et le néant* (Paris: Librairie Gallimard, 1943), p. 77.

[74]

self whom Kierkegaard sought, who has lost the whole world but not himself.

The treatment of "abandonment" (*délaissement*) (Heidegger's *Geworfenheit* or the *facticité* of *L'Être et le néant*) is, though in a different way, equally disturbing; for it is clear from the example which he discusses that Sartre himself, despite his profession to the contrary, is using "subjectivity" in the narrower, not the broader, sense. A young man has to choose between staying at home with his mother, otherwise alone, and going to join the Free French in England. The point is, of course, that the boy must create his own values in his own situation—he can only do what he is and be what he does; no supernatural values appear in the heavens to guide him. Granted; but in the description of the situation a significant factor is omitted: the relation between the boy *and* his mother which will or will not bear this or that decision, a decision of hers as well as his and possibly of theirs. True, the boy's choice is this very concrete particular choice which no pre-existent values can determine. But he does not therefore choose as if, suddenly and out of all relation to the freedom of any other person, he alone had to decide. He is, as the existentialists say, already flung into a world, a world that involves his relation to his mother and hers to him; and his decision to leave or stay with her is inseparably bound to her acts, past and present, as well as to his own. It is the history of two people together that is at issue. Yet, existentially seen, the son chooses not only in his situation but alone in it. The "deeper sense" of subjectivity is easily forgotten.

Finally, in dealing with the objection that the existentialist cannot criticize the morality of others, Sartre replies that, besides the criticism in terms of bad faith, the existentialist can also demand that one choose for the sake of freedom itself, not only for one's self but generally, since "the freedom of one involves the freedom of others." Again, this is

[75]

superficially logical; but, like the general statement about subjectivity or the good for all, it is too easy; and nothing in the much more detailed analysis of *L'Être et le néant*, or in the novels and plays for that matter, bears it out. One must admit, as we shall see in the discussion of Sartre's political philosophy, that, *given* as foundation the general principle of freedom for its own sake, of human liberty in general as an absolute value, one can construct upon it an ingenious and, at least superficially, consistent philosophy of revolution. But the question remains: how from the solitary creator of a world who dares to bear his lonely freedom, who decides "alone, unjustifiable, and without excuse," one can deduce so easily an agent of universal freedom, a proletarian inheritor of the French libertarian tradition. In short, as put in the *Humanism* essay, the whole discussion of the transition from or relation of individual to general subjectivity, or of personal to political freedom, though it may be good propaganda, avoids or distorts the philosophic issues at every turn.

3

The analysis of "Le Pour-autrui" in *L'Être et le néant* is more honest, as well as more exhaustive, and reveals more clearly, I think, the blind spots of this particular existentialism, as well as its insights. It is an extremely detailed account, of which we can here indicate only some of the more significant or striking features.

Experience, for Kant, Sartre reminds us, was organized ultimately as *my* experience—no bridge to another self was provided in the Kantian analysis. The temporal flow of consciousness that forms the material of the inner sense I *know*, in psychology, as a phenomenal self, much as I know the material of the outer sense, in physics, as an ordered world of objects. But only my own self is so accessible to me; for only my consciousness is open to the inner sense. So I can find no access to another subject. I cannot know it empirically; and a noumenal self, a self-in-itself, I cannot know for anyone, myself or another. Thus the Kantian criticism leaves the way open for solipsism. However universal may appear the "understanding" or the "reason" with which Kant is dealing, it is still an abstract, skeletonic I who possess such understanding or such reason, an I for whom there is, as far as one can see, no meeting ground for any contact with others of his kind. Moreover, Sartre demonstrates, neither "realistic" nor "idealistic" solutions of this problem in the nineteenth century were adequate; for each of these philosophies needed, inconsistently, to call the other to its aid. Such a Kantian idealist as Schopenhauer, for example, has simply to *take* the other subject as a reality, which, properly, his systematic idealism should not allow. And such scientific philosophies as positivism, on the other hand, have, just as illegitimately, to infer another self as an *ideal* construct, when all they *know*, strictly speaking, is a set of inferences from one set of sense-data to another such set, with no intervening "self" at all. Even granting them such inconsistencies, moreover, neither school could refute solipsism on a more than probable basis, whereas, according to Sartre, only some kind of certainty could really effectively banish this philosophical hobgoblin.

Some progress has been made, however, Sartre believes, in the analyses of Husserl, Hegel, and Heidegger, and he considers their attempted solutions as a preface to his own. Husserl did try, he says, to show that I am what I am essentially in relation to another ego. But the relation involved was both external and intellectual and so, remaining doubly within the sphere of the merely objective or merely probable, failed to touch the core of the problem. Hegel had gone further, Sartre thinks, in that he understood the relation between two selves to be internal. In fact, the description of master and slave in the *Phenomenology of Mind* is something of a sacred text for Sartre's own interpretation; for his theme is essentially that of the attempted but uneasy absorption of one consciousness into another, or their reciprocal making of each other through the destruction of each other. Yet in its outcome Hegel's interpretation, too, fails; for the relation which it portrays, though internal, is still intellectual, it is still the *knowledge* of self by self that he struggles with. And, above all, such knowledge, like all his dialectic, is envisaged in terms of a whole that for Sartre is quite illusory and irrelevant—the one all-embracing system of Absolute Mind is as fantastic to Sartre as it was to Kierkegaard. Heidegger, finally, has at least abandoned the cognitive basis of the problem and has rightly taken it out of its falsely intellectual setting in both Husserl and Hegel. We can never, Sartre points out, know another self other than probably—as, in fact, we know any object in our world; and hence, if the question is put in terms of knowledge, we can never eliminate solipsism as a possible answer. Heidegger's existential analysis is correct in putting the whole question on a different footing. But, on the other hand, Heidegger's theory of "existing-together," Sartre feels, fails much more radically than, say, the Hegelian master-slave view. It generalizes about the togetherness of all of us but misses the concrete problem of *this* man's contact with *that* man; and, if Heidegger had squarely met that more concrete issue, he might have found something quite different from a simple togetherness constitutive of one person's meeting with another.

That something different Sartre himself then proceeds to look for in an extended argument for his own theory: in an account of what, in his view, does happen when I realize, not cognitively but immediately and absolutely, the existence of another person, another free center of another world, which yet in some way enters or overlaps or, as we shall see, annihilates mine. It is the fact of another's look-

[78]

ing at me, Sartre believes, that reveals the existence of another subject—not the mere physical presence of a pair of eyes directed my way but the whole transformation of my world that the look behind those eyes implies. For in that experience of being looked at by another I find myself becoming, not the transcendence I otherwise feel myself to be, but a mere object, a body appearing thus and thus in someone else's world. For myself, my body is the sheer givenness of my being-in-situation, the closest and concretest reality in the widening range of contingencies that, on the factual side, sets the limits and direction of my nature. For the other person, whom I find looking at me, I become *only* a body, a thing within his horizon, as "objective" as the chair I am sitting on or the cup of coffee I am drinking.[5]

The revelation of the other existence observing me is, for Sartre, like my awareness of my own existence, a direct experience, a "slightly enlarged *cogito*"; and by this experience, not cognitive in its nature but, just for that reason, immediate and final, the possibility of solipsism is once and for all eliminated:

The Cartesian *cogito* does nothing but affirm the absolute truth of a fact: that of my existence; similarly, the slightly enlarged *cogito* we are using here reveals to us as a fact the existence of another and my existence for another. That is all we can say. Thus my being-for-another, like the emergence into being of my consciousness, has the character of an absolute event.[6]

But the other existence which thus reveals itself is, at the same time, annihilation of myself as subject; and such an annihilation I am bound to try by every means in my power to overcome. Therefore, between myself as subject and the other who sees me as object, between my freedom and its destruction in another's possession of me, there arises a circle

5. There is also, in this account, a third "ontological dimension" of body, in which I also, as the other does, apprehend my body as a thing.

6. Sartre, *L'Être et le néant*, p. 342.

of conflicts which constitutes, according to Sartre, the whole pattern of possible intersubjective relationships. "Conflict is the original sense of being-for-another."[7]

Sartre introduces this theory with two examples. Suppose that I am sitting in a park and see another person walking near me. Suppose the other person to be reading a book. He and his book are then as wholly "objects" as, say, the tree-on-the-grass or the fountain-in-the-square. Man-reading-book, like the other things in their places, is a self-contained unit, holding no obvious threat to me or my world. But suppose the stranger's eye, instead of being fastened attentively to his page, is wandering over the paths and borders, so that I may at any moment find he is looking at me. Such a shift in his attention would suddenly reveal me as an object in *his* world—and by this possibility the whole world of *my* consciousness, the world as *I* have ordered it, is threatened with disorganization and destruction. The awareness of such a possibility causes, Sartre says, an "internal hemorrhage" of my world: it bleeds in the direction of the stranger. Hence, for Sartre, the appearance of the other person in my world is the occasion for possible, if not actual, disruption of that world; and fear, the natural reaction on my part to such a possibility, would seem to be my original relation to him in such circumstances.

Or, Sartre continues, suppose I am listening at a keyhole, whether out of jealousy, spite, or whatnot—the motive is irrelevant. And suppose I suddenly feel myself, in turn, observed. All at once I feel the eyes of an observer on me and turn to find him looking at me. All at once, instead of being engaged as a free agent in a project of my own, I am revealed to myself, as to the unexpected observer, as an object in his view. My transcendence is, in turn, transcended by him as free agent; I am what *he* makes of me, not what I make myself. I recognize the indignity and absurdity of

7. *Ibid.*, p. 431.

my position, stooping awkwardly at a keyhole; I am that laughable or despicable thing, an eavesdropper; and I am ashamed. But what makes my eavesdropping shameful *is* its discovery (see the innumerable scenes, in Fielding, for example, of servants discovered listening at doors). It is the transformation of a project into a posture that makes the posture ridiculous. And, in general, it is the transformation of myself from free agent shaping my own world to body seen by another that is the source of shame. Hence Sartre's explanation, already quoted, of original sin: it is the revelation of my body as a mere body that makes me ashamed; and that shame is at the root of the sense of sin. This conception of the existential meaning of the body and, in particular, the naked body is illustrated in *The Age of Reason*, for example, in Marcelle's confession to Mathieu that she is pregnant. Mathieu's nakedness is appropriate if his body is touching hers in the usual gestures of love-making. But when she, clad, surprises him, naked, with such a disturbing and unexpected revelation, their amatory routine is broken, and he feels himself humiliated as well as annoyed by her information. The important point for Sartre, of course, is that, whatever example one chooses, such an experience implies an onlooker and that, in fact, conversely, the existence of an onlooker implies shame. Fear and shame are, for him, the two proper and immediate reactions to the intrusion of another person into my world.

The only alternative to shame or fear, if the onlooker threatens to make me a mere subject by his looking, is to turn and look at him. In that case I in my pride (*orgeuil*) threaten him with extinction. Hence the principle of conflict—all relations between myself and another are, existentially, a battle to the death. Either he, a person, transcends my transcendence and makes a thing of me, or I in my prouder freedom transcend and so annihilate his liberty. Or, rather, that is how the conflict looks; but it never ends in

[81]

victory for one or the other. Even murder cannot change the fact that the victim, by having existed, has threatened and limited my liberty. There can be no knockout blow or even a decision, only round after round of a bout that never stops—and never starts either, for it is a continuous and unbreakable circle.

There is, it is true, an *apparent* escape from my objectification by another in the substitution of vanity for shame. In vanity I accept my object-status and try, by the kind of object I am—clever or beautiful or the like—to *affect* the other person in his very freedom. But this is only another case of "bad faith"—that is, of the false objectification of my freedom—which can find no satisfactory fulfilment; for what I thus create is an *image* of myself in the other person. To find that image, I must, in turn, objectify him; and what I find there is only disillusionment, for I find a false image that is not what I am but what I seemed to him. My own essence fails still of the objectification that I thought it could find. I am destroyed as surely by my own vanity as I might have been by my antagonist's pride.

There is, then, at least in terms of this analysis, no escape from the alternative of fear/shame or pride as fundamental to my relations with another. There are, however, further variations within these two types of relationships which Sartre proceeds to analyze. They are all aspects of sexuality, which, for Sartre, is not merely psychologically but "ontologically" essential to human existence. Not the contingent facts of my having this or that sex or these or those particular habits of expressing my sexual nature but the fact that, quite generally, I am "a sexed being" is what he finds existentially so important. The basic variants in the expression of that fundamental nature he describes, again, in terms of the original duality in all relations between individuals: either I become object for another subject, or another becomes object for me as subject.

[82]

There is, Sartre points out, no special reason for starting with any one of these relationships, since the whole constitutes a circle. In point of fact, he begins with the first of the two that we have mentioned and with its exemplification in *love*. Love, according to Sartre, is the wish to be loved: that is, I as object want to take hold of the very liberty of the other by becoming myself—i.e., my object-self—the source of his values, the only meaning of his freedom. That is why, Sartre says, the lover always wants to know if the beloved would rob for him, murder for him, etc. Love is the attempt of the self-seen-as-object to absorb another's freedom by making itself the highest reality, the ground of all significance for that freedom. When such absorption threatens to fail (and it cannot succeed, since two are two, not one), the lover tries to bring about his end by *seduction*, by making himself a "fascinating object." This is, Sartre says, a basic type of language, not in the narrow sense of verbalization, but in the primitive sense of expressiveness in general. Such expressiveness is, however, still doomed to failure by the very logic of the situation. The lover wants the beloved to love him: he wants as object to "make worth living" the life of the beloved as free subject. But suppose he succeeds. Then the beloved loves the lover. That is to say, the beloved himself turns object in relation to the lover as subject. So the original character of the relationship is contradicted by its own fulfilment. Love by its very nature carries with it its own frustration.

Faced with such frustration, I may try again, desperately, this time not simply to absorb the other's liberty to my own being as fascinating object, but to reduce myself to *nothing* but an object, so completely that I appear even to myself as object before the other's total freedom. Such an attempt is *masochism*, in which I love the shame of my object-character and try in every way to stress and to increase it. At the same time, my shame is, though cherished, felt as guilt: "I

[83]

am guilty to myself, because I consent to my absolute alienation, guilty to the other, because I furnish him the occasion of being guilty, that is, of missing radically my freedom as such."[8] But this attempt again carries its frustration within it; for, no matter how much I make myself an object, it is *I* by *my* free effort who do so. In fact, masochism, Sartre says, like every vice, "loves its own frustration." It is "a perpetual effort to annihilate the subjectivity of the subject in making the other assimilate it and .... this effort is accompanied by the fatiguing and delicious consciousness of frustration, to the extent that it is the frustration that the subject ends by seeking as its chief end."[9]

If the attempt to accept my own object-character has no satisfactory issue, then I may try as subject to reduce the other to mere object. *Indifference* is an attempt of this sort. I take the others whom I meet solely in their functional capacities as ticket-collector, elevator man, receptionist, and what not, and hence deny implicitly their individual existence as personalities. Yet this is an unsatisfactory solution, since there is the perpetual danger of the man in the park— one of these functional automata may at any moment destroy my illusion of superior solitude by looking at *me*.

More aggressively, I may seek to annihilate, rather than merely to ignore, another's freedom in *sexual desire*. Desire, for Sartre, is the endeavor to produce the *incarnation* of another subject, that is, to ensnare the other's freedom in the flesh, to reduce him not to body in general or to an object in the instrumental sense but to this very concrete present flesh. The means to this end is myself to become flesh in order, by physical contact, to reduce the other person to the same purely fleshly existence. Therefore, the achievement of desire lies, in Sartre's view, not in the fulfilment of the sexual act itself but in the caress, in which the hand, becom-

8. *Ibid.*, p. 446.
9. *Ibid.*, p. 447.

[84]

ing flesh, makes flesh of breast or thigh, or the whole body, made flesh, makes flesh of the other's body, and so seems, momentarily at least, to transfigure and transcend his freedom. But desire, too, contains its own frustration. The sexual act itself and, in general, "la volupté sexuelle proprement dite" are, in Sartre's view, purely contingent aspects of human nature, dependent on particular given physiological structures and so on. And the pleasure that accompanies the achievement of such an act is irrelevant to, even destructive of, the profounder meaning of desire. For pleasure, at first immediate, produces a reflective consciousness of pleasure, which becomes itself an end; and as I seek my own pleasure I am distracted from, and lose the aim and awareness of, the other's incarnation, which is the proper function of desire. In another way, too, desire is frustrated. As desire to *possess* the other, it tries to do more than make flesh of the other's freedom, it tries actively to lay hold of the other's "incarnate consciousness." Here I cease being flesh and try, *using* my body, to seize and appropriate the other's liberty; and here desire, in turn, gives way to sadism:

This situation implies the breaking of the reciprocity of incarnation which was, precisely, the proper end of desire: the Other may remain troubled; he may remain flesh *for himself*; and I may understand him; but it is a flesh I no longer grasp by my flesh, a flesh which is no longer anything but the *property* of Another-as-object and not the incarnation of Another-as-consciousness. So I am *body*, . . . in the face of flesh. I find myself practically back in the situation from which I was just trying to escape through desire, that is, I try to use the object-Other to demand of him an account of his transcendence, and, just because he is *all* object, he escapes me with *all* his transcendence. I have even, once more, lost the clear understanding of what I am seeking, and yet I am engaged in the search for it. I take and I discover myself in the course of taking, but what I take in my hands is *something else* than what I wanted to take; I sense it and I suffer, but without being capable of saying what I wanted to take; for, troubled as I am, the very comprehension of my desire escapes me; I am like a dreamer who, waking, finds himself engaged in clenching his hands on the edge of the bed without recalling the nightmare that induced his gesture. It is this situation which is at the origin of sadism.[10]

The object of sadism, Sartre says, is "immediate appropriation." The sadistic, like the desiring, consciousness wants to identify another's freedom with his flesh. But the sadist seeks that end without himself becoming flesh and without giving up the instrumental character of the other-as-object:

He wants the nonreciprocity of sexual relations, he rejoices in being power, free and appropriating, in the face of a freedom that is captured by the flesh. That is why sadism wants to make the flesh present *differently* to the consciousness of the Other: it wants to make it present by treating the Other as an instrument; it makes it present through pain. In pain, in short, facticity invades consciousness, and, finally, the reflective consciousness is fascinated by the facticity of the nonreflective consciousness. There is then indeed an incarnation through pain. But at the same time pain is produced *by instruments*; the body of the torturing For-itself is only an instrument for giving pain. So the For-itself can from the beginning give itself the illusion of taking possession instrumentally of the freedom of the Other, that is of drowning that freedom in the flesh, without ceasing to be he who *provokes*, who beats, who seizes, etc.[11]

What sadism seeks to produce is the obscene, that is, flesh revealed to an observer without desire. But that aim, too, is thwarted, since it is the very freedom of the other that the sadist tries to seize, and that freedom constantly escapes him. Quoting the closing scene of Faulkner's *Light in August*, Christmas looking up at his murderers, Sartre says:

Thus this explosion of the look of Another in the world of the sadist makes the meaning and end of sadism collapse. At one and the same time sadism discovers that it was *that liberty* it wanted to enslave and realizes the vanity of its efforts. Here we

10. *Ibid.*, pp. 468–69.
11. *Ibid.*, pp. 469–70.

[86]

are once more returned from *the-being-who-looks* to *the-being-who-is-looked-at,* we do not leave the circle.[12]

Not even *hate,* as a last desperate remedy, can break these bonds; for, as we said, murder itself, impelled by hate as the attempt at total destruction of the other person, fails of its object. The other *has* been and has been free; that encroachment on my total liberty I cannot cancel or forget. The circle, then, of conflict on conflict is still unbroken; it is a treadmill from which, in my endeavor to approach another's freedom, I can never find escape.

4

This is, at least, facing the question squarely. But as an exhaustive account of human relationships it is, to say the least, depressing. To lessen our despair a little, we might look again at Sartre's exposition and, in particular, at the examples with which he introduces "the look of the other." My relation to another is revealed, as we have seen, in the moment at which, sitting in a park, I find a stranger looking at me or at least about to look at me. But surely this is a highly artificial example on which to base an analysis of personal relations. An individual confronts another; but both are abstracted by the public nature of the place from the personal setting in which each of them, in fact, lives his life. So it is not the two as living human beings who face each other but the facsimiles of humanity who are, in Heidegger's phrase, together in the "one." I may, indeed, conjecture from the look of the stranger something of his personal reality; but in that case I project him in imagination into his world, a world of other human beings to whom he stands in as intimate relation as do I to those whom he, too, can only guess at. In the anonymous togetherness of so-called "career women" in a genteel restaurant, for instance, what emerges as real behind their mutual silence is the lack that

12. *Ibid.,* p. 477.

each one feels of the organic relationships beyond herself that could give substance to what is otherwise an empty freedom. That feeling is not, I think, only—though it is in part—a surrender to convention, a desire to be what society and instinct combine in urging against the deeper claims of freedom. It is, beyond that, the sense of wanting the completion of one's self in others which is just as genuine in human consciousness as is the ultimate privacy which existentialism prefers to stress. For an account of the need of human beings for one another the myth of Aristophanes in the *Symposium* is at least as valid as are Sartre's four hundred pages.

It is, in other words, some such sense of the original togetherness of particular human beings as that myth conveys that is lacking in Sartre's analysis. Perhaps, if Kierkegaard's inwardness is taken as the whole of human personality, the principle of conflict as the "original sense of my relation to another" does follow. But to take that solitary inwardness as the whole already involves an abstraction amounting to distortion. The difference of me from every other person is, indeed, a unique, perhaps even the most essential, aspect of my nature. But existentialism is a philosophy which boasts that it takes seriously the living, temporal growth of the person, growing through the transcendence into his peculiar future of his particular past. Surely, then, it is strange that such a philosophy should ignore altogether the growth of that unique sense of difference itself; for consciousness itself, for all its inwardness, evolves, after all, out of a pattern of organic relationships from the total dependency of the unborn child on its mother, through the gradually lessening dependence of the infant and young child. In that process others are essential to the individual neither as threats to his own liberty nor as mere objects in his world but rather as the very foundation of that world itself. Even if it could be said in general that, with adolescence and maturity, conflict becomes the fundamental relation of child to parent, the original togetherness of the family has surely influenced significantly the character of that conflict itself.

Again, Sartre's other example is equally suspect. His description of shame and vanity are indeed illuminating as descriptions of just those passions; and, what is more, it is a surprising gap in earlier philosophic accounts of the passions that they so frequently fail to take account of shame as an extremely important and central emotion. Yet neither Sartre's examples nor his object-subject theory suffices to make credible the view that shame is *the* original expression of my relation to others, that fundamentally and exclusively I see myself as bodily nakedness before all others as spectators—and destroyers. One could maintain, for example, with at least as much show of reason, that the original relation of myself to another lies in the recognition of another *like* myself, who enriches and completes my freedom rather than threatens to annihilate it. Such an experience may be infrequent; so in the ordinary course of our daily lives is shame. But it may, for all that, reveal the scope and richness of my freedom as essentially as shame reveals its instability.

Moreover, the same limitations of example and of theory carry through Sartre's whole analysis. The descriptions of masochism and sadism are extremely telling; in part even, notably in the account of the caress, there is something to be said for the discussion of desire. But, in general, the endeavor so completely to divorce the "existential" import of sex from its biological foundation produces a strangely twisted picture. For instance, if there is, as Sartre thinks, existential significance in the fact of sexuality as such, there is also, I suspect, "existential" meaning in the distinction between masculine and feminine—a distinction, it is true, not necessarily coterminous with the physiological differentiation of the sexes. Goethe's "das ewig Weibliche" is one part German sentimentality and one part a male egoist's excuse to himself for a succession of Friederikes; but I must

[89]

reluctantly confess a suspicion that there is something more to it as well. At any rate, the avoidance of such merely "contingent" differences gives a certain artificiality to the framework of Sartre's discussion.

What is worse, within that framework some of his analyses are so inadequate as to be almost tours de force—in particular, the account of love, where both definition and argument fall most obviously short of his material. This is not the place, nor have I the skill, to elaborate an alternative theory; I can only point again to the Platonic Aristophanes, to Diotima's account of immortality, or to the myth of the *Phaedrus*. What the lover of Aristophanes' story wants is not just to be loved but to be made whole again, to become wholly himself in union with the other from whom an unnatural cleavage has divided him. Or again, what the lover of the *Phaedrus* craves is not simply the love of the beloved but the growth of his soul's wings, which only the beauty of the beloved, by recalling beauty itself, can give him. And in that process the soul of the beloved as well as the lover is nourished and ennobled. So regarded, love is not so much the desire to be loved as it is the sense of one's completion in another through shared insights and aspirations. In existential terms, the transcendence of the lover here neither transcends nor is transcended by another but becomes aware of itself, i.e., becomes itself, through the participation of the very freedom of another in his freedom; and, in turn, the other's transcendence—the project that he is—expands and ripens in its way through similar participation. Were there no such mutuality, no such growth of two souls through the reciprocal enrichment of each other's freedom, the dilemma of the Sartrean lover might indeed obtain—though it is, like much in Sartre, almost too logical to match reality. But if the major premise is false, so is the conclusion; and, surely, no one but the most faithful disciple could deny its falsity. Sartre's account of sadism is striking in its genuineness; it is, after all, the account of a member of the Resistance who presumably knew extremely well the ways of the Gestapo. Besides, as we shall see in more detail later, it is just this kind of revelation of humanity dehumanized that Sartre excels in. But his *amour* smacks of the bad French novels that Victorian heroines were wont to hide under their pillows.

Sartre does consider the possibility of some community of human beings, some positive union between them, beyond the principle of conflict. An "us," he says, a *nous-objet*, does arise when two individuals, engaged in the inevitable conflict with each other, find themselves jointly the *object* of an onlooker. In this case the third person objectifies them both, and in their mutual danger they find indirectly, but only indirectly, a kind of union. That is, I suppose, the kind of unity Sartre is drawing in "La Chambre" between Eve and her mad husband, a unity against the hostility and horror of her bourgeois father. It is also the kind of unity that determines, according to him, the nature of class-consciousness. Not the common needs or sufferings of the poor but the discovery of the rich man's looking on at them creates an "oppressed class." But the individuals within that class are still bound only by the tensions of love, hate, desire—that is, for Sartre, by conflict. I do not know whether this is an adequate account of class-consciousness; it is certainly a brilliant description of the occupied countries, where the hatreds and recriminations of peacetime political life were for once overridden by the annihilating presence of the outsider.

A "we," on the contrary, a *nous-sujet*, Sartre thinks, occurs only accidentally; for instance, when I ride in the Métro, the signs "exit" and "entrance" by implication, and the figures and faces of the other passengers explicitly, show me that I am along with others in a world made by and for many. But my togetherness with the others, while it creates a strange temporary "we," is not essential to my personal existence. It is a passing phenomenon that leaves no permanent mark on me. In fact, of course, it is the very strangeness of the passengers to one another that gives this kind of incidental "we" its peculiar character.

And is this all? As far as Sartre can see, it is; but there are some things that he does not see. True, each man alone must make himself what he is to be. Only he can make his world the absurd order, the ordered absurdity, that it is; and of that terrible freedom no one can rob him. But there are, I think, at least two points at which the Chinese wall of subjectivity is broken.

The particular given situation out of which I make my world is not itself entirely private; and, though it becomes a world primarily for me, there are still, even in our society, some occasions on which it becomes a world genuinely for us. One can see this still, for instance, in some agricultural operations, such as a threshing, where the demands of the facts themselves produce for a few hours a genuine unity in the men who deal with them. Obviously, those occasions were more frequent in the old days of barn-raisings, hand-haying, and so on; and obviously, too, there are in modern urban society no such events at all. Here, indeed, there is the "one" and the despairing freedom of the Mathieus who would not be lost in it—and perhaps no more. But if we have lost those activities—part work, part ritual—in which men genuinely stand together to wrest the goods they need from a co-operative, yet unwilling, nature, we have no right, in consequence, to call our sophisticated loneliness a universal condition of mankind.

On the side of freedom itself, moreover, rather than of its contingent conditions, there is, now and then, escape from the solitary confinement of the self-against-all-others. Even if most human contacts are, as contacts within the "one," bereft of reality, sometimes surely (as we suggested earlier) an individual comes somewhere upon what he can only call, lamely enough but rightly, "his own kind of person"—one

[92]

who can share, if only for moments, his own projection of himself, his own liberty, without threatening it or being threatened by it. Existentialists like to find philosophical significance in common idiom. What does it mean, then, to "see eye to eye" with another? Surely, that he and I can look at one another directly in a more than physical sense, as two centers of liberty which can be free together, not endangering each other but united through understanding of our similar aims. Granted, that such direct communication between individuals occurs only seldom; but, if it has ever happened at all to any one anywhere, that is enough to break the charmed circle of observer and observed, threatener and threatened.

One more word, not so much on *L'Être et le néant* as on Sartre the philosopher-artist. The analysis of the contact between individuals as an endless struggle of each personality, by destroying the other, to escape its own destruction, involves, as we have seen, giving to sex a place of central importance in the description of personal existence. But, beyond that, taking Sartre's writing as a whole, one senses something more, perhaps deeper than his extreme individualism, certainly somehow allied to it: a love of exploring to the limits the extreme or perverse in human nature. The preoccupation with the *voyeur* in such stories as "Eristrostrate" or "Intimité," for example, or the study of Daniel in *The Age of Reason*, or such incidents as Ivich cutting her hand have, like most things in existential literature, obvious, often too obvious, philosophical implications. But, conversely, the philosophy seems to feed on perverseness. Even to the analysis of normal sexual phenomena in *L'Être et le néant* there is a twist that makes it extremely subtle perhaps, but subtly mistaken as well. The plays of Sartre, Eric Bentley says, are philosophic melodrama rather than tragedy and, for that very reason, are more "maturely modern" than would-be tragedies, which fail to suit the "nontragic" temper of our

[93]

time.[13] Something similar is true even of the more technical expressions of Sartre's philosophy, as well as of his novels and stories. Whatever it is that makes our age "nontragic," that it is which makes existential philosophy, like existential drama, suit it so well. Only I cannot feel so cheerful about the whole thing as Mr. Bentley seems to do. Of philosophy, the most abstract of the linguistic arts, as of drama, one needs to remember what Synge says in his essay "The Vagrants of Wicklow":

In all the healthy movements of art, variations from the ordinary types of manhood are made interesting for the ordinary man, and in this way only the higher arts are universal. Beside this art, however, founded on the variations which are a condition and effect of all vigorous life, there is another art—sometimes confounded with it—founded on the freak of nature, in itself a mere sign of atavism and disease. This latter art, which is occupied with the antics of the freak, is of interest only to the variation from ordinary minds, and for this reason is never universal.[14]

If existentialism suits us, it is as much our failure as existentialism's success.

13. See Eric Bentley, *The Playwright as Thinker* (New York: Reynal & Hitchcock, 1946), chap. vii, Sec. IV, pp. 232–46.
14. J. M. Synge, *In Wicklow, West Kerry, and Connemara* (London: George Allen & Unwin, Ltd., 1919), p. 12.

CHAPTER FIVE

FRENCH EXISTENTIALISM AND POLITICS: THE NEW REVOLUTIONARY

1

To the very long analysis of the circle of conflicts there is a very short footnote: "These considerations do not exclude the possibility of a morality of deliverance and salvation. But this can be attained only at the end of a radical conversion, of which we cannot speak here."[1] I have no means of knowing what sort of deliverance this is; but it is reasonable to assume that Sartre is referring to the political theory and practice of his group, which, starting with the Resistance, has since become increasingly articulate. Here the stress on the individual's loneliness is joined with, or even subordinated to, social and political solidarity, with revolution rather than mere personal rebellion as its end. Here the subject made object by another identifies himself with the whole class of people so oppressed and seeks to liquidate the oppressor qua oppressor by creating a free society, in which there are no slaves and masters but all men stand together as persons mutually respecting one another. This is currently, through numerous articles in Les Temps modernes, the most publicized and, for the existentialists themselves apparently, the most serious, or at least the most urgent, aspect of their doctrine. Yet, despite the logical link through his theory of class-consciousness,[2] the Sartrean political

1. Jean-Paul Sartre, L'Être et le néant (Paris: Librairie Gallimard, 1943), p. 484.
2. See p. 91, above.

theory seems, at first sight, a strange addition to the existential view of the individual and the values, individually upheld, individually created, by which he lives. In other words, in looking at the political theory of French existentialism, one is continually faced with the question which we have already mentioned in connection with the *Humanism* essay. *How*, in this highly individualistic theory of human nature, does the liberty of one involve the liberty of all? Or, in the light of our examination of *L'Être et le néant*, how does one reconcile a principle of the mutual respect of free beings for one another's freedom with the principle that each man's freedom reciprocally implies the repression of every other?

Quite apart from logic and philosophy, the first answer to that question is a historical one. French existentialism did not begin with the Resistance. Sartre's pre-war publications, like *Le Mur* and the *Esquisse d'une théorie des émotions*, differ in no fundamental way from the later developments of his theory. But existentialism as a popular movement in French philosophy and, in particular, existentialism as a political philosophy did grow into their present prominence out of the peculiar stresses of the Occupation and the peculiar pattern of life—that is, of torture and death—in the Underground. That pattern illuminated, more dramatically and more insistently and on a national scale, what the inner self-torment of a Kierkegaard had revealed a century earlier: the utter loneliness of each of us in moral crisis and the essential union, almost the identity, of that loneliness and the freedom that we find in it. Man makes himself, but only in secrecy and solitude—publicity is betrayal or illusion. This contrast, in the Occupation, takes the extremer shape of paradox: the more oppressed we are externally, the freer we can be in our own decisions, in our single lives. So Sartre says in "The Republic of Silence":

We were never more free than during the German occupation. We had lost all our rights, beginning with the right to talk. Every day we were insulted to our faces and had to take it in silence. Under one pretext or another, as workers, Jews, or political prisoners, we were deported *en masse*. Everywhere, on billboards, in the newspapers, on the screen, we encountered the revolting and insipid picture of ourselves that our oppressors wanted us to accept. And, because of all this, we were free. Because the Nazi venom seeped even into our thoughts, every accurate thought was a conquest. Because an all-powerful police tried to force us to hold our tongues, every word took on the value of a declaration of principles. Because we were hunted down, every one of our gestures had the weight of a solemn commitment. The circumstances, atrocious as they often were, finally made it possible for us to live, without pretense or false shame, the hectic and impossible existence that is known as the lot of man.[3]

And, what is more, the objects of each man's decisions in such circumstances have a peculiar significance for the revelation of man's destiny in general. Kierkegaard's problems were often, as he himself says, "bagatelles" to the external observer. Should he or should he not use a pseudonym? Should he or should he not pay a call on the long-lost (and very-long-indifferent) Regina? But each act of every Frenchman under the Occupation implied a much more dramatic and much more universal question. Sartre continues:

Exile, captivity, and especially death (which we usually shrink from facing at all in happier times) became for us the habitual objects of our concern. We learned that they were neither inevitable accidents, nor even constant and exterior dangers, but that they must be considered as our lot itself, our destiny, the profound source of our reality as men. At every instant we lived up to the full sense of this commonplace little phrase: "Man is mortal!" And the choice that each of us made of his life and of his being was an authentic choice because it was made face to face with death, because it could always have been expressed in these terms: "Rather death than. . . . ." And here I am not speak-

3. Sartre, "The Republic of Silence," translated by Ramon Guthrie, in *The Republic of Silence*, compiled and edited by A. J. Liebling (copyright 1947 by A. J. Liebling), pp. 498–500. Reprinted by permission of Harcourt Brace & Co., Inc. The quotations given in this chapter comprise the whole of the essay.

ing of the élite among us who were real Resistants, but of all Frenchmen who, at every hour of the night and day throughout four years, answered NO. But the very cruelty of the enemy drove us to the extremities of this condition by forcing ourselves to ask ourselves questions that one never considers in time of peace. All those among us—and what Frenchman was not at one time or another in this situation—who knew any details concerning the Resistance asked themselves anxiously, "If they torture me, shall I be able to keep silent?"

Kierkegaard's "70,000 fathoms," Heidegger's "being to death," are interesting philosophic conceptions; but here is the human actuality that has given a new dimension and a new vitality to their eccentric, if brilliant, insights:

Thus the basic question of liberty was posed, and we were brought to the verge of the deepest knowledge that man can have of himself. For the secret of a man is not his Oedipus complex or his inferiority complex: it is the limit of his own liberty, his capacity for resisting torture and death.

Whatever one may think of the theoretical correctness of the existentialists' view of the individual and of its consistency or otherwise with their political philosophy, one must qualify such criticism by recognizing the genuineness of this hard-won insight, and by conceding that those of us who have not known the daily threat of death or torture have ulti-mately no right to speak against it. "It is characteristic of the French," Edmund Wilson wrote in his otherwise ex-cellent review of Sartre in the New Yorker,[4] "that the de-struction of French institutions should have seemed to them a catastrophe as complete as the Flood and caused them to evolve a philosophy which assumes that the predicament of the patriotic Frenchman oppressed by the German occupa-tion represented the situation of all mankind." Perhaps so; it may be that French existentialism more than other phi-losophies expands a unique situation into a universal theory.

4. Edmund Wilson, "Jean-Paul Sartre, the Novelist and the Existentialist," New Yorker, August 2, 1947, p. 61.

But Wilson would scarcely be the last to admit that something similar is true of philosophers generally, as it is of artists, and that for each philosophy the unique experience from which the resultant system has grown as much confirms as invalidates the theory itself. And in this case our fortunate ignorance of the situation must make us, at any rate, hesitant in our judgment of the consequent theory. Perhaps it was unique only in the sense of historical accident; perhaps it was unique, rather, as the existentialists believe, in its revelation of the very limits of human liberty. Thucydides, too, saw the effect of one war on one people and saw in it the situation of all mankind; that is, at least, good precedent for the existentialists' procedure.

What makes the Resistance most significant for the politics of the French school, however, is not simply the secret, yet dramatic, loneliness of each Underground worker, but the conjunction of solitude with solidarity in this invisible army. In the Resistance it was true, undeniably, that each man, deciding alone and of himself, did decide for all. So Sartre's essay concludes:

To those who were engaged in underground activities, the conditions of their struggle afforded a new kind of experience. They did not fight openly like soldiers. In all circumstances they were alone. They were hunted down in solitude, arrested in solitude. It was completely forlorn and unbefriended that they held out against torture, alone and naked in the presence of torturers, clean-shaven, well-fed, and well-clothed, who laughed at their cringing flesh, and to whom an untroubled conscience and a boundless sense of social strength gave every appearance of being in the right. Alone. Without a friendly hand or a word of encouragement. Yet, in the depth of their solitude, it was the others that they were protecting, all the others, all their comrades in the Resistance. Total responsibility in total solitude—is not this the very definition of our liberty? This being stripped of all, this solitude, this tremendous danger, were the same for all. For the leaders and for their men, for those who conveyed messages without knowing what their content was, as for those who directed the entire Resistance, the punishment was the same—imprisonment, deportation, death. There is no army in the world where there is such equality of risk for the private and the commander-in-chief. And this is why the Resistance was a true democracy: for the soldier as for the commander, the same danger, the same forsakenness, the same total responsibility, the same absolute liberty within discipline. Thus, in darkness and in blood, a Republic was established, the strongest of Republics. Each of its citizens knew that he owed himself to all and that he could count only on himself alone. Each of them, in complete isolation, fulfilled his responsibility and his rôle in history. Each of them, standing against the oppressors, undertook to be himself, freely and irrevocably. And by choosing for himself in liberty, he chose the liberty of all. This Republic without institutions, without an army, without police, was something that at each instant every Frenchman had to win and to affirm against Nazism. No one failed in his duty, and now we are on the threshold of another Republic. May this Republic about to be set up in broad daylight preserve the austere virtues of that other Republic of Silence and of Night.

Like the experience of liberty in enslavement, the experience of "total responsibility in total solitude" is here undeniably genuine. In the Resistance the freedom of one *did* involve, immediately and heroically, the freedom of many. It was as himself *and* as a Frenchman that each man had to ask, "If they torture me, shall I be able to keep silent?" —just as, conversely, it was himself as much as France that each collaborator betrayed. But it is here, too, that the theoretical question becomes insistent. The situation of the Resistance, in which each man does indeed decide for everyone, was made a consistent whole by the dramatic force of its actual existence. But when this situation is elevated to the status of an abstract system, what link is there to bind, theoretically, the solitude with the responsibility, the one with the all? The picture of the individual vis-à-vis his torturer remains as the human, historical foundation of Sartre's theory of the relation to another as conflict. But what conception of community, country, or humanity provides, in existential theory, the logical equivalent for the other side of the Resistant's solitary and dangerous decision?

2

Before looking at Sartre's explicit formulation of political or social theory, however, we should notice, short of such general theoretical statements, a kind of analysis of human types or behavior patterns to which existentialism lends itself with conspicuous success. That is illustrated, for example, as we have already seen, in such analyses as those of vanity, sadism, or masochism in *L'Être et le néant*. The broader social implications of some of these discussions—as of the concept of total, yet perilous, freedom on which they are founded—are ample. In part, for example, Sartre's interpretations of sadism and of hate are utilized in his "Portrait of the Anti-Semite,"[5] or in Simone de Beauvoir's discussion of revenge and punishment in "Eye for Eye."[6]

Take such a paragraph as this, in the latter essay:

"He will pay for it"—the word is telling; to pay is to furnish an equivalent for what one has received or taken. The desire for equivalence is expressed more exactly in the famous *lex talionis* or law of retaliation: "An eye for an eye, a tooth for a tooth." Doubtless, this law retains, even at present, a magical after-taste; it tends to satisfy some unknown, somber god of symmetry; but first and foremost it corresponds to a profound human requirement. Once I heard a member of the *maquis* telling how he had retaliated on a National Guard who had been guilty of torturing a woman. "He understood," he concluded, soberly. This word, which is frequently used in this violent and elliptical sense, is a declaration of the principle of vengeance, a statement of its profound intention. No abstract conception is involved here, but exactly what Heidegger is talking about when he speaks of

5. Sartre, "Portrait de l'antisémite," *Les Temps modernes*, I, No. 3 (December, 1945), 442–70. This essay also appeared in translation as No. 1 in *Partisan Review*'s pamphlet series.

6. Simone de Beauvoir, "Oeil pour œil," *Les Temps modernes*, I, No. 5 (February, 1946), 813–30. Translated by Mary McCarthy in *Politics*, July–August, 1947, pp. 134–40.

[101]

"understanding"—an operation by which our whole being realizes a situation; you understand a tool by using it; you understand a torture by experiencing it. The butcher feels, in his turn, what the victim felt, but this in itself cannot remedy the original evil. It is not enough for the suffering to be relived or revived; the totality of the situation must be revived also. The butcher, who saw himself as sovereign consciousness and pure freedom confronting a wretched tortured thing, is now a wretched tortured thing himself, experiencing the tragic ambiguity of the human condition. What he has to understand is that the victim, whose abjection he now shares, shared something else with him too— the very privileges he thought he could arrogate to himself. And he does not understand this intellectually, in a speculative manner. He realizes concretely the turnabout of situation; really and concretely, he reestablishes the state of reciprocity between human consciousnesses, the negation of which is the most fundamental injustice. An object for others, every man is a subject to himself, and he lays the sharpest claim to being recognized as such.[7]

Sartre's theme of the self-defeating character of the passions, moreover, and, more broadly, of the double-faced paradoxical character of our freedom itself recurs in Mlle de Beauvoir's explanation of the contradictory nature of both vengeance and its abstract substitute, punishment. In the case of vengeance:

What is involved is nothing less than the coercion of freedom— the terms are contradictory. Yet there can be no true revenge except at this price. If the butcher should decide, without external pressure, to repent his error, and even were to go so far, in the zeal of remorse, as to retaliate on himself, he might possibly disarm revenge, but he would not gratify it, because he would remain pure freedom, and in the very sufferings that he might inflict on himself voluntarily he would still, in spite of himself, be making mock of his victim. What is required is that he should feel *himself* as victim, *he* should undergo violence. But violence, by itself, is not enough either; its only point is to give rise in the guilty person to an acknowledgement of his true condition; the very nature of freedom, however, makes the suc-

7. *Politics*, p. 136.

cess of this dubious. Violence can be an inducement, a temptation, but never an absolute compulsion. What we really want is
to cast a spell on the enemy's freedom, to seduce it like a woman:
the alien consciousness must remain free with regard to the content of its acts; it must freely acknowledge its past faults, repent,
and despair; but an external necessity has to force it to this spontaneous movement. It must be led from without to extract from
itself feelings nobody could impose upon it without its own
consent. This contradiction is the reason that revenge's aims can
never be satisfied.[8]

In punishment there is a more complex problem, for we
have no longer the concrete struggle of one freedom against
another but the substitution of an abstract pattern in which
the condemned man, though he must suffer in his own flesh
and his own spirit, is at the same time, for his judges, rather
the symbol than the actuality of the wrongdoer. This difference of punishment from vengeance was particularly evident,
Mlle de Beauvoir says, in the trial of Pétain:

In vengeance, the man and the criminal are blended in the
concrete reality of a unique freedom. By being able to discern in
Pétain both a traitor and an old man, condemning the one, par-
doning the other, the High Court merely demonstrated, up to the
hilt, one of the tendencies of social justice: it does not view the
guilty man in the totality of his being; it does not engage in a
metaphysical struggle with a free conscience that a body of flesh
and bone imprisons; it condemns him insofar as he is a substract
and a reflection of certain bad acts. The punishment, therefore,
takes the form of a symbolic display, and the condemned man
comes close to being seen as an expiatory victim, for, after all, it
is a man who is going to feel in his consciousness and his flesh
a penalty intended for that social and abstract reality—the guilty
party.[9]

But such duality is inevitable, since it is implicit in the very
nature of human action and human freedom:

.... every attempt to counterbalance the absolute event which
is a crime manifests the ambiguity of the condition of man, who

8. *Ibid.*   9. *Ibid.*, p. 137.

is simultaneously freedom and thing, unity and dispersion, isolated by subjectivity and yet coexistent with other men in the world's bosom—hence all punishment is one part defeat. But love and action too—quite as much as hatred and revenge—always involve a defeat, and that does not stop us from loving and acting, for we have not only to ascertain our condition; from the heart of its ambiguity we must choose it.[10]

Or again, in the "Portrait of the Anti-Semite," Sartre applies partly his conception of sadism, partly the existential conception of the free project itself to a difficult social problem. Wilson likens this essay to some of the portraiture of the eighteenth-century encyclopedists. It should also be distinguished from the eighteenth-century intellectualist tradition that still, in its senile decay, dominates most of our discussions of "prejudice," "intolerance," and the like. Sartre is not, he makes it clear at the start, discussing "anti-Semitism" as an opinion; for the anti-Semite is not just a man who, besides being a good husband and father, an astute politician, or what not, happens in addition to hold such and such regrettable or mistaken opinions. He is a man who, in no relation at all to the whole problem of evidence and the opinions formed from it, has chosen hate as his way of life. It is the character of that basic choice, not a list of humanly ridiculous or historically plausible opinions, that has to be understood. For Hume and his pragmatic-positivist descendants there is no essential difference between reasonable opinion and prejudice, only prejudice is an opinion founded on a narrower, rather than a wider, range of evidence. So if, with the nice, sensible cool-headedness that all men possess when beyond the spell of rabble-rousers, the intolerant are shown the scientific evidence for tolerance, they will, of course, alter their "antisocial" attitude to a more "constructive" one. Logically, scientific opinion is only broadminded prejudice, and prejudice is narrowness of

10. *Ibid.*, p. 140.

opinion; the exposition of relevant evidence will, as a matter of course, substitute the more for the less desirable of the two. As against such a highly abstract, totally unrealistic, and therefore, I suspect, almost totally ineffective conception, the incisiveness and penetration of Sartre's "Portrait" is a welcome, even if not a cheering, antidote. The anti-Semite, he says, has, first and foremost, chosen hate. He has chosen "to live in the impassioned mode":

It is not rare that one chooses a passionate life rather than a reasonable one. But that is usually because one loves the *objects* of the passion: women, glory, power, money. Since the anti-Semite has chosen hate, we are obliged to conclude that it is the impassioned *state* that he loves. Usually, this kind of affection does not please at all; he who passionately desires a woman is impassioned because of the woman and in spite of the passion; one scorns passionate reasonings, which try to demonstrate by every means opinions that love or jealousy or hate have dictated; one scorns passionate distractions and what has been called "mono-ideism." That is, on the contrary, what the anti-Semite has chosen first. But how can one choose to reason falsely? Because one yearns for impermeability. The sensible man seeks, groaning; he knows that his reasonings are only probable, that other considerations will occur to call them in doubt; he never knows very well where he is going; he is "open," he can pass for hesitant. But there are people who are attracted by the permanence of stone. They want to be massive and impenetrable, they do not want to change: where could the change take them? It is a matter of an original fear of self and of a fear of truth. And what terrifies them is not the content of the truth, which they do not even suspect, but the very form of the true, that object of indefinite approximation. It is as if their own existence were forever in suspense. But they want to exist all at once and immediately. They do not want acquired opinions, they want innate ones; because they are afraid of reasoning, they want to adopt a way of life where reasoning and investigation have only a subordinate role, where one never seeks except for what one has already found, where one becomes nothing but what one was already. There is no such thing except passion. Only a strong emotional commitment can give a lightning certainty; it alone can

[105]

hold reasoning by the leading-strings, it alone can remain impermeable to experience and subsist through a whole life. The anti-Semite has chosen hate because hate is a faith; he has chosen, at the outset, to devaluate words and reasons. How much at ease he feels now; how futile and slight seem to him the discussions on the rights of the Jew: he is situated from the first on a different plane. If he consents, by courtesy, to defend his point of view for a moment, he lends but does not give himself; he simply tries to project his intuitive certainty onto the plane of discourse. I quoted earlier some "mots" of anti-Semites, all absurd: "I hate the Jews because they teach want of discipline to servants; because a Jewish furrier robbed me; etc." Don't think the anti-Semites deceive themselves in the least about the absurdity of these replies. They know their arguments are slight, contestable; but they are amused by them: it is their adversary who has the duty to use words seriously because he believes in words; as for themselves, they have the *right to* play. They even like to play with arguments because, by giving clownish reasons, they throw discredit on the seriousness of their interlocutor; they are of bad faith and delight in it, for with them it is a question not of persuading by good arguments but of intimidating or disorienting. If you press them too briskly, they close up, they let you know with a haughty word that the time for arguing has passed; it is not that they are afraid of being convinced; they fear only that they may look ridiculous or that their embarrassment may have a bad effect on a third person whom they want to attract to their party. If, then, the anti-Semite is, as everyone has been able to observe, impermeable to reason and to experience, it is not because his conviction is strong; but rather his conviction is strong because he has chosen in the first place to be impenetrable.[11]

Moreover, in his impenetrability, he has, Sartre continues, chosen to be terrible: to be the objective image of himself that inspires fear in others. He has chosen mediocrity—again because his mediocrity can be cherished as a thing, not fought for in hazardous freedom; for he possesses the mystic heritage of blood and soil against the corrosives of a rootless intelligence. And in that possession he has found an objective Good, which he shares equally with all Frenchmen, all

11. Sartre, "Portrait de l'antisémite," p. 448.

Aryans, or the like, by their opposition to the detested Jew, who is, as the object of hate, the embodiment of pure evil. In this "manichaeism" there is no need to search out, in dread, the significance of one's values, to wrest a precarious good from entanglement in ill: good and evil are given, to destroy the evil is the mission of the good. So, finally, the anti-Semite appears as destroyer and sadist—since his good demands as its expression the suffering and, finally, the destruction of the victim that he has marked as evil. In all this it is the fixity, the objectivity of himself and his good, that he has chosen. True, he has chosen hate, which is a passion not a thing; but his hate carries him beyond himself, takes him from the peril of self-questioning, from doubt, dread, and risk, to certainty:

> He chooses, finally, that the Good be ready-made, beyond question, beyond attack; he dares not look at it for fear of being led to contest it and seek another. The Jew is here only a pretext: elsewhere one makes use of the Negro, elsewhere the yellow races. His [the Jew's] existence simply allows the anti-Semite to stifle his anxieties in the egg by persuading himself that his place in the world has always been marked, that it awaits him, and that he has, by tradition, the right of occupying it. Anti-Semitism, in a word, is fear of the human condition. The anti-Semite is the man who wants to be pitiless rock, furious torrent, destroying thunder; anything but a man.[12]

There are, of course, Sartre says, so-called "anti-Semites" who do not conform to this pattern. There are all those who have taken on the attitude of "not bearing the Jews"—or the Negroes or who not—merely to seem to be somebody to their associates. He mentions a man who, otherwise entirely undistinguished by conduct or conversation, has always been known to his acquaintance as "unable to abide the English": so his presence becomes noticeable by everybody's avoidance of the hated subject. This character, in its anti-Semitic form,

12. *Ibid.*, p. 470.

Sartre himself has depicted with ghastly success in the long concluding story of *Le Mur*, "L'Enfance d'un chef." The complete emptiness of the boy's and young man's life, the lack of any significant passion in it, is compensated for at last when he has got away with his refusal to shake hands with a Jew at a party. There was no overpowering hatred back of his act; it was, if anything, just a capricious attempt to be different; but it succeeded; his host on their next meeting apologized; and he was established as someone: someone who detests the Jews.

In all these instances, of course, it may be just the shrewdness of the particular writers, without much regard to their existentialism, that makes the analyses apt or interesting. That would seem to be so, for example, of some of Sartre's comments in his editorial introduction to the United States issue of *Les Temps modernes:*

The system is a great external apparatus, an implacable machine which one might call the objective spirit of the United States and which over there they call "Americanism"; it is a monstrous complex of myths, of values, of formulae, of slogans, of symbols, and of rites. But it would not do to think that it is deposited in the head of every American as Descartes's God has deposited the primary notions in the mind of man; it would not do to think that it is "refracted" in their brains and in their hearts and that it there determines at every moment emotions and thoughts which are its rigorous expression. It is, in fact, outside; it is *presented* to the citizens; the most skilful propaganda presents it to them ceaselessly but never does more than present it: it is not in them, but they in it; they struggle against it or accept it, they stifle in it or transcend it, they submit to it or reinvent it every time, they give themselves up to it or make furious efforts to evade it; in every way it remains external to them, transcendent, since they are men and it a thing. There are the great myths, that of happiness, that of progress, that of liberty, that of triumphant maternity; there is realism, optimism; and then there are the Americans who at first are nothing, who grow among these colossal statues and disentangle themselves as best they can in the midst of them. There is the myth of happiness; there are those spellbinding slogans which advise you how to be happy as quickly as possible; there are the films with happy endings, which every evening show life in rose color to harassed crowds; there is that language, laden with optimistic and profligate expressions, "having a good time," "enjoy," "life is fun," etc.—and then there are those men who are pursued even into the most conformist happiness by an obscure malaise that does not know what to call itself, those men who are tragic for fear of being so, by that total absence of the tragic in themselves and around them. . . . .

Nowhere can one find such a wedge between men and myths, between life and the collective representation of life. An American said to me at Berne: "The trouble is that each of us is haunted by the fear of being less American than his neighbor." I accept that explanation; it shows that Americanism is not a simple myth that a skilful propaganda could bury in people's heads but that every American reinvents it, gropingly, every minute; that it is at once a great external form which rises at the entrance to the port of New York, opposite the Statue of Liberty, and the daily product of unquiet liberties. There is a dread of the American in the face of Americanism; there is an ambivalence of his dread, as if he were asking himself at one and the same time: "Am I American enough?" and "How shall I escape Americanism?" A man, in America, is a certain simultaneous answer to these two questions; and every man must find his answers alone.[13]

Yet even here there is an echo of the existential view of freedom, of the conception of man's making himself out of his history rather than that of history's making him; and one can at least say that, frequently, as against the more abstract, more easily generalizing interpretations of "social psychology," "progaganda analysis," and the like, the concreteness, the very individualism, of the existential view does lend itself exceedingly well to certain—limited if you like, but penetrating—kinds of human and social portraiture.

13. Sartre, "Présentation," *Les Temps modernes*, I, Nos. 11–12 (August–September, 1946), 194–95, 196–97.

The problem of connecting, logically, the private and public aspects of existentialism becomes acute, however, if we
look at its supporters' explicit statements of political and
social theory. The *locus classicus* for this theory, at present
writing, is Sartre's pair of articles on materialism and revolution in *Les Temps modernes*.[14] The first essay considers a
series of contradictions in materialism, notably, in dialectical
materialism, the contradiction, as Sartre sees it, between the
unique concrete wholes envisaged by dialectic and the abstract, quantitative relations with which scientific materialism is bound to deal. So, for example, Engels is incorrect, he
says, in his assertion that physics moves from quantitative
to qualitative concepts: it moves only from quantity to quantity. Even Einsteinian physics deals wholly in external and
quantitative relationships; and, what is most essential, even
Einsteinian physics, like all science, deals with the abstract
conditions of the universe in general, not, like dialectic, with
the growth of a living concrete totality. Sartre admits freely
the usefulness, for revolutionary purposes, of the materialist
myth—or at least its usefulness in the past. Yet both as philosopher and as revolutionary he questions the long-term
efficacy of such a "monster" and proceeds, in the second
essay, to construct an alternative theory of revolution with,
in his view, a sounder, nonmaterialistic basis.

The revolutionary, according to Sartre, must be oppressed,
but essentially oppressed, that is, oppressed in such a way
that only a radical change in the structure of the society can
relieve his oppression:

What the American Negroes and the bourgeois Jews want is
an equality of rights, which does not in any way imply a change
of structure in the regime of property; they simply want to be

14. Sartre, "Matérialisme et révolution," *Les Temps modernes*, I, Nos.
9 and 10 (June and July, 1946). Selections from these two essays also appeared in translation in the July–August, 1947, *Politics*.

assimilated to the privileges of their oppressors, that is, at bottom they seek a more complete integration.

The revolutionary is in a situation such that he can in no way share those privileges; it is by the destruction of the class that is oppressing him that he can obtain what he demands. That means that the oppression is not, like that of the Jews or Negroes, considered as a secondary and, as it were, lateral characteristic of the social regime but that it is, on the contrary, constitutive. The revolutionary is, then, at once a victim of oppression and a keystone of the society which oppresses him; more precisely, it is in so far as he is oppressed that he is indispensable to that society.[15]

That means, secondly, that he is a worker: it is those who "work for the ruling class" who are indispensable to the society in their very oppression. Such is his situation; the third characteristic of the man, according to Sartre, is that he goes beyond his situation—*il la dépasse*—toward a radically different situation, which it is his aim to create. A philosophy of revolution, then, will be a philosophy "in situation" but also a program of action beyond that situation. In particular, it will substitute a new conception of value for that of the ruling class; and, since this ruling class founds its domination on its conception of the rights of man, that is of the divine right of the bourgeois ruler to oppress the proletarian worker, it will be not an assertion of rights but a denial of them. Hence, presumably, the appeal of materialism, since it substitutes a natural conception of the human species for the bourgeois pretense of human dignity, which is only the dignity of ruler-person against worker-thing. But, by so doing, it negates all values, whereas what the revolutionary seeks is a new conception of values, one which goes beyond the present situation, which envisages goods to be created in revolution rather than imposed by reaction.

To describe adequately the revolutionary attitude, then, Sartre says, four points are needed:

15. *Les Temps modernes*, No. 10, p. 2.

(1) that man is unjustifiable, that his existence is contingent in that neither he nor any Providence has produced it; (2) as a consequence, that every collective order established by men can be transcended [*dépassé*] in the direction of other orders; (3) that the system of values current in a society reflects the structure of that society and tends to preserve it; (4) that it can, therefore, always be transcended toward other systems, which are not clearly perceived because the society which they express does not yet exist but which are anticipated and, in one word, invented by the very effort of the members of the society to transcend it.[16]

These points, he continues, neither materialism nor idealism provide. Materialism with its rigid causality leaves no room for freedom—and the transcendence of one value-situation toward another, which is essential to the revolutionary, *is* freedom: "This possibility of moving away from a situation [*décoller*] to take a point of view on it (point of view which is not pure knowledge but indissolubly understanding and action)—this is precisely what we call 'freedom.' "[17] Idealism does no better, he believes, since, while recognizing subjectivity, it fails to acknowledge, what is equally important, the hardness of fact—the stubbornly existent obstacles which the revolutionary, in his very freedom, has set himself to overcome. Moreover, idealism is, for Sartre as clearly as for the orthodox Marxist, merely the attempt of the ruling class to cloak its self-interest in grand phrases. The correct account is one different from either of these:

A being contingent, unjustifiable, but free, completely plunged into a society which oppresses him but capable of transcending that society by his efforts to change it, that is what the revolutionary man claims to be. Idealism mystifies him in that it binds him with its already given rights and values; it masks his power of inventing his own paths. But materialism also mystifies him, by robbing him of his freedom. The revolutionary philosophy

16. *Ibid.*, p. 12.
17. *Ibid.*, p. 13.

must be a philosophy of transcendence [*une philosophie de la transcendence*].[18]

So the revolutionary philosophy turns out to be the philosophy of freedom—not just the philosophy of those who seek freedom but the philosophy of the very free act itself, the philosophy of transcendence; that is, though Sartre does not here call it so, it turns out to be existentialism. And what is more, as *the* philosophy of freedom, it turns out, according to Sartre, to be *the* philosophy of man in general. It starts, indeed, in one class, that of the workers—but a bourgeois doubtful of his own class values may come to accept it; and, besides, it seeks, despite the probable need of bloodshed, not so much to destroy the ruling class as to join workers and former rulers in a community of men, to make them equally free. So it is not, like either materialism or idealism, a myth used by one faction or another but a statement of the nature and action of the free man as such: the revolutionary, by his very choice of revolution, becomes "the man who wishes that man freely and totally assume his destiny."[19]

Such, in brief outline, is Sartre's philosophy of revolution. There is, of course, an obvious plausibility in the equation of the free act with the revolutionary act—there is a striking parallel, if not a logical equivalence, between the existential concept of transcendence, of choice in, but beyond, a concrete situation, and the revolutionary's transcendence of his social and political situation in his very grasp of it. But, despite the striking rightness of some of Sartre's incidental observations (see, for instance, the passage quoted on pp. 6–8 on the relation of mechanical cause to human aims and choices), the theory as a whole has a certain artificiality about it: it is, again, somehow too logical in the wrong places. The philosopher's love of a neat logical construct has several times

18. *Ibid.*, pp. 13–14. I have translated *dépasser* by "transcend." The French term *transcendence* occurs only in the final phrase "philosophy of transcendence."
19. *Ibid.*, p. 30.

led to a failure of Sartre the artist: as in *The Flies*, which is topheavy with existential theory, or even in *The Unburied Dead*, where the possible variants on the genuinely moving theme of death and torture are so exhaustively and conscientiously explored that the result is something more like a psychologist's card-index than a tragedy.[20] But here it is the philosopher himself who is guilty of too much neatness with too little reality or, in the jargon of the trade, too much coherence with too little adequacy.

This is apparent at several points. In the first place, one is likely to ask one's self, as Sartre himself asks of the Communist: What of the revolutionary after the revolution? The philosophy of the free man in its political aspect is the philosophy of transcendence as such, of going beyond the present society to create a new one. At present, in Sartre's picture, it is the dichotomy of oppressor and oppressed that motivates such transcendence. But what of the free man in the free society? If he is still free, he still transcends his situation to a new one; he is still, by definition, a revolutionary, but against what? Against freedom itself? That is absurd. The reply might be, I suppose, that revolutionary philosophy is, as Sartre says, "in situation": it is thought now directed to a currently pressing and significant end. But Sartre has insisted, against the Communists, that a *philosophy* of revolution must be at once immediately prac-

20. Cf. Edmund Wilson's comparison of Sartre with Steinbeck in the review already quoted (p. 58): "Like Steinbeck, Sartre is a writer of undeniably exceptional gifts: on the one hand, a fluent inventor, who can always make something interesting happen, and, on the other, a serious student of life, with a good deal of spirit. Yet he somehow does not seem quite first-rate. A play of Sartre's, for example, such as his recent 'The Unburied Dead'—which is, I suppose, his best play—affects me rather like 'The Grapes of Wrath.' Here he has exploited with both cleverness and conviction the ordeal of the French Resistance, as Steinbeck has done that of the sharecroppers; but what you get are a virtuosity of realism and a rhetoric of moral passion which make you feel not merely that the fiction is a dramatic heightening of life but that the literary fantasy takes place on a plane which does not have any real connection with the actual human experience which it is pretending to represent."

tical and universally true; otherwise it is not a philosophy but a mere myth, a myth which may by its falsity ultimately stifle revolution itself. Sartre's philosophy, by contrast, must be not a lie however noble, but *the* truth of *la condition humaine.* In that case one is bound to try at any rate to envisage his free man in settings beyond the present one, to imagine him *in* the future that alone gives substance and significance to his freedom. And there one can see him only as a lost revolutionary: as one who *has* created by his free act the society embodying, as far as a society can, the values in which he has chosen to believe, yet whose very nature as free demands that he once more deny *these* values in his transcendence, that he go beyond the very liberty for which he has lived his life and risked his death to something beyond liberty itself—and beyond that again, and so forever. In endless regress as such there is no contradiction, but there is in this one; for here revolution for freedom implies revolution against freedom. And back of that logical impasse there is a hint at least of a much profounder difficulty in existential theory—liberty as such, in its bare logical essence, does not appear an adequate replacement for more substantive conceptions of value.

In the description of the present, prerevolutionary situation, moreover, there are, for the American reader at least, equally disquieting limitations. Sartre's sketch of the oppressed worker's situation is an account of a capitalist society in which an acute and well-defined class-consciousness is much more highly developed than it is with us. If one is already a Marxist and has already interpreted the legend of American democracy in terms of its economic origins, one can satisfactorily explain the lack of a stable class-consciousness out of those same economic conditions—and proceed to try to create one. But Sartre's description is, presumably, not deduced from any theory; and, as a straightforward "phenomenological" account, it simply does not fit our case.

The *fact* of oppression and exploitation exists, of course—it is probably just about as hard for a West Virginia miner's son to grow up to anything but the mines—where he works hard and dangerously for other men's profits—as it is for Sartre's French laborer to be anything but the victim of exploitation that his father was before him. But if the American worker sometimes feels himself cheated, it is only because, as Sartre says of the Forty-eighters, he wants particular conditions bettered within the society: here, however—and this is the important point—not because he accepts oppression but because he cannot seriously conceive of himself as oppressed at all; because he feels that by some absurd accident he has been, for the moment, deprived of the privilege which must and shall accrue to *all* Americans—the right to possess, to raise further and further the famous standard of living that distinguishes us among the peoples of the earth. Sartre is probably quite right in saying, in his editorial on America, that the American myth is not so much lived by as lived under, that every American tries constantly, with an odd insecurity, to re-win and reassert its efficacy for himself. Yet, despite this relation of distance between the people and their faith, it is still, for most of them, the only faith they know or can imagine; and for such a faith (as several contributors to *Temps modernes's* United States issue have stressed) a rigid division of classes, clearly recognizable from both sides of the cleavage, can hardly be said to exist. Here, it seems to me, much more than in the relation of his thought to the French Resistance, Sartre has indeed tried to build a general theory upon a situation whose geographical and historical limits seriously impair its universal validity.

These are both disturbing limitations in the Sartrean theory; but there is a more serious and more sweeping objection, which we anticipated at the outset of this chapter. Sartre's political theory and his analysis of the individual, using as they do the same central concepts—situation, freedom, transcendence—form an interesting pair of parallels. Is there, or is there needed, any bridge, any logical connection, between the two, or can the parallelism stand as such? That there is need for such a connection can, I suppose, hardly be questioned; for any theory of the state and society, no matter how wide its field of reference, rests ultimately on and follows from some theory of the nature of the individual, if only on a denial that there *is* an individual. That Sartre tries, in his own case, to make such a connection is also clear; and it is, I am afraid, equally evident that he fails to make it with cogency or conviction.

The crux of the matter lies in the concept of *solidarity*. The revolutionary must be distinguished from the rebel. He does not seek liberation for himself alone, for that would involve only absorption into the ruling class. He seeks it for his whole class, even, at last, for all mankind. In his description of class-consciousness in *L'Être et le néant* Sartre has represented the oppressed group as united, indirectly, for such joint action, by their awareness of the oppressor as onlooker.[21] Directly, however, they are still bound by the ties of conflict only, which alone forms the dynamic of one individual's relation to another, whether within or beyond his class. The conception of the oppressor as onlooker and therefore as destroyer of subjectivity is likewise involved, in part, in the *Temps modernes* essays. But there are at least strong hints that this alone is not enough: that something more than an indirect *nous-objet* is needed *within* the oppressed class itself if one is to achieve solidarity rather than anarchy, a common revolution for freedom rather than the sporadic rebellion of the individual against his individual tyrant. Look at two passages in the second essay:

We have seen . . . . that the revolutionary act is the free act *par excellence*. Not at all of an anarchist and individualist freedom;

21. See p. 91, above.

[117]

in that case, as a matter of fact, the revolutionary, by his very situation, could only claim more or less explicitly the rights of the privileged class, that is, his integration to the higher social strata. But since he claims at the heart of the oppressed class and for all the oppressed class a more rational social status, his freedom resides in the act by which he demands the liberation of all his class and, more generally, of all men. It is, at its source, recognition of other liberties, and it demands to be recognized by them. Thus it places itself from the beginning on the plane of solidarity.[22]

This is, at first sight, a clear and logical statement of the revolutionary position; but its Achilles' heel appears in the sentence: "It is, at its source, recognition of other liberties, and it demands to be recognized by them." Whence this recognition of other "liberties"? From where in the circle of conflicts can it spring? The threat of the oppressor and the stand of the oppressed against him one can see as a variant on the basic pattern of the subject-object conflict. But a tie of mutual recognition, first among the oppressed and ultimately among all mankind—that one finds one's self, within the framework of Sartre's existentialism, unable to conceive. Within that framework, as Sartre himself has said, "respect for another's freedom is an empty phrase" (le respect de la liberté d'autrui est un vain mot).[23]

The second passage is, if anything, more weasel-worded:

A revolutionary philosophy must take account of the plurality of liberties and show how each one, even while being liberty for itself, can be object for the other. It is only this double character of freedom and objectivity that can explain the complex notions of oppression, of struggle, of frustration, and of violence. For one never oppresses but one freedom; but one cannot oppress it unless, in some respect, it lends itself, that is, unless, for the Other, it presents the exterior of a thing. Thus one will understand the revolutionary movement and its project, which is

22. Sartre, "Matérialisme et révolution" (second half), p. 26.
23. Sartre, L'Être et le néant, p. 480.

to make society pass by violence from a state wherein liberties are alienated to another state founded on their reciprocal recognition.[24]

Here we have the explicit statement of the oppressor-oppressed/subject-object equation. It is in terms of conflict and, as far as one can see, conflict only that the revolutionary recognizes the "plurality of liberties." But suddenly out of this grim picture "one understands the revolutionary movement and its project, which is to make society pass by violence from a state wherein liberties are alienated to another state founded on their reciprocal recognition." From what human situation, from what new and marvelous source in the depths of a subjectivity otherwise so lonely, so closely and so constantly endangered, does this balm of reciprocal recognition flow? Without it the whole theory of revolution as the philosophy of human liberty, as man's call "to his total destiny," collapses into unreality. Yet in the existential view of the individual there is no place for such recognition and therefore, one is bound to conclude, no foundation on which to build the political theory which Sartre himself has sketched.

This is, as a matter of fact, apparent at some points, even in the less general and therefore, on the whole, more satisfactory discussions that we quoted earlier. For example, the passage on torture and vengeance by Simone de Beauvoir continues:

An object for others, every man is a subject to himself, and he lays the sharpest claim to being recognized as such. Everybody knows, for example, how many fights in crowded places start with a bump or an accidental kick: the person that gets jostled inadvertently is not simply a body, and he proves it—he defies the other person with a word, a look; finally he hits him. The respect he is exacting for himself each of us claims for his near ones and finally for all men. The affirmation of reciprocity in interhuman relations is the metaphysical basis for

24. Sartre, *Matérialisme et révolution* (second half), p. 28.

[119]

the idea of justice. This is what revenge is striving to reestablish against the tyranny of a freedom that wanted to make itself supreme.[25]

And this expansion of one's own claim to all humanity is further elevated by Mlle de Beauvoir into a universal moral principle:

.... there are cases where no redemption seems possible, because the evil encountered is an absolute evil; and when this happens, we find the point of view of charity is no longer acceptable, for we think that absolute evil exists. You can excuse every misdemeanor and every crime, even, by which an individual asserts himself against society; but when a man deliberately sets about to debase man into thing, he lets loose a scandal on earth which nothing can make amends for. This is the only sin against man there is, but once it has been brought to pass, no indulgence is allowable, and it is man's business to punish it.[26]

That this *is* absolute evil, the ultimate and only sin against mankind, I heartily agree. Yet, it is, at the same time, by Sartre's account,[27] the only possible relation of one human being to another: either I try, in desire or sadism, to make another into a thing and so am guilty toward him; or I debase my own subjectivity to thinghood, as in love or masochism, and so sin against myself. That is, perhaps, only to say we are all sinners. So we are. But if, where there is sin, there is sometimes no redemption, in general there is—or at least the hope of it. And such hope can come, in this case, only if respect for some other and so, indirectly at least, for all others can break the circle of perpetual conflict. Mlle de Beauvoir says that it does so; yet her assertion stands against,

25. De Beauvoir, *op. cit.*, p. 136.
26. *Ibid.*, p. 139.
27. Simone de Beauvoir's analysis of intersubjective relations seems to differ in some respects, as I have said above, from that of Sartre. It does not, however, to judge from the fragments that I have seen, differ in the essential respect relevant to our discussion here, i.e., it does not provide a "reciprocal recognition" of two equally free beings for one another's freedom. It presents, rather, a hierarchy of transcendences, in which each person makes himself object for his "peer."

[120]

rather than within, existential theory. Her description of the conflict that constitutes vengeance is brilliant; but the transference to the level of general morality slips in, like the "mutual recognition" of Sartre's essay, without due introduction or explanation. Or again, the same is true of Sartre's own remark in the "Portrait of the Anti-Semite": "A man who finds it natural to denounce men cannot have our conception of the human."[28] What is "our conception of the human"? Where does it suddenly come from? One does not expect French ideas, any more than Frenchmen, to travel about without a *carte d'identité*, or at any rate a passable counterfeit thereof.

28. Sartre, "Portrait de l'antisémite," p. 451.

CHAPTER SIX

JASPERS AND MARCEL: THE NEW REVELATION

1

THE storm around existentialism rages mostly about Sartre and the French atheistic school, of whom even Heidegger is said to have said "Good God! I never intended *that!*" But on the periphery of the movement are writers—apart even from the Barthian theological heirs of Kierkegaard—for whom God has not yet died and for whom, moreover, even the loneliness of the Kierkegaardian self is, at least ostensibly, conquered by the discovery of immediate communication between selves. So, it seems, the stress on personal existence may serve the lonely vision of God, as in Søren Kierkegaard; or it may stem from the denial of God but issue in a self equally solitary, as in Sartre or Heidegger. Or it may, as in the Protestant Karl Jaspers or the Catholic Gabriel Marcel, involve a recognition both of faith in God and of direct communication with other finite selves as necessary elements in personal existence itself. The only permutation I have not seen stated is an existential philosophy affirming direct communication while denying God. This is, I think, historical accident rather than logical necessity; for it appears to be the result of coincidence rather than of logic that both Marcel and Jaspers insist on (in Jaspers' terms) both communication and transcendence. That faith in God does not imply direct communication we know from Kierkegaard, for whom *indirect* communication is a necessary consequence of the kind of subjectivity that alone leads to true faith. That the acknowledgment of communication, conversely, does not imply a transcendent faith, one can only guess—for example, from the weakness of the attempted union of the two in Jaspers or Marcel. But, lacking such a philosophy, we may fill out historically, if not logically, the outlines of actual, rather than possible, existential theories by examining some aspects of the Protestant and Catholic varieties, respectively, in Jaspers and Marcel.

Both these men belong to the increasing group of those who lament the mechanization of personality that has accompanied the mechanization of industry. In an essay on contemporary irreligion, published in *Être et avoir* in 1935,[1] Marcel attacked three contemporary philosophies: the idealistic, the technical, and what one may call the "vital," that is, the philosophy which identifies the human in man with the merely living. Of these, it is the second which is most important and most dangerous. As Marcel sees it, the principal characteristics of a technical view of the world are that it understands things only in terms of some hold (*prise*) that human agents have on them, some way of manipulating them; that such techniques of manipulation and, consequently, the world itself appear perfectible—even natural catastrophes are looked on as unaccountable flaws in the machinery which we have not yet rectified but of course will ultimately; and that, in the light of this way of regarding things, man himself becomes for himself only an object of such techniques, knowing himself only by reflection as another object to handle and to perfect when he fails to run right. The moral results of this world-view are, for Marcel, conspicuous and deplorable. Since the "interior life" is minimized by such an externalizing attitude, human aspirations are reduced likewise to their minimum, i.e., to the mechanical pursuit of instantaneous pleasures—which Marcel calls "le Anglo-Saxon having a good time." (The epithet seems a bit unfair to the Puritan tradition!) Moreover, if good is

1. Gabriel Marcel, *Être et avoir* (Paris: Fernand Aubier, 1935), pp. 259–95.

reduced to mere momentary pleasure, neither is the real nature of evil understood in our technical age. Marcel's point here is rather provocative, though, of course, not new: that it is just the notion of an *imperfect* world whch is combined in our time with the denial of radical evil. The world as God made it was perfect, yet it had a devil in it. The world of the machine has its breakdowns, but it also has no mysteries and therefore no flaws which cannot be righted by new and improved techniques. Evil really beyond our power to conquer does not exist. There are grievous social consequences, too, in Marcel's view, of the technical philosophy. By reducing man to another object of his own technique, we have, he thinks, turned society from a genuine community into an aggregate of deadened, pleasure-seeking, pain-shunning units that bear no inner spiritual relation to one another. Marcel's model for a genuine community, of course, is the church, where faith forms the spiritual bond that unites its members. And the common source for all these ills of our time is our forgetfulness of the only part of man that makes him man—his soul. It is to save this better part of our nature from its present decline that he turns to the analysis of personal existence as a philosophic leitmotiv.

Jaspers directed a more extended and rather celebrated polemic against technocracy in *Die geistige Situation der Gegenwart*, which appeared as No. 1000 in the "Göschen" pocket series and was also published in English (if one can call it such) under the title *Man in the Modern Age*.[2] Though it covers a number of fields—everything from war to education—its theme is extremely simple: it is an attack on the *Massemensch*. In every area—political, social, and cultural—Jaspers finds the failure of our age in the human analogies to mass production: in the leveling-down of human differences and therefore of the only significant human achievements, to fit the cheap and shoddy pattern of the mass-pro-

2. New York: Henry Holt & Co., 1933.

duced average man. This does not mean, despite his talk of such things as a "genuine war" or a "true aristocracy," that Jaspers is opposing political democracy. The "genuine war" I cannot claim to understand—like Marcel's genuine religious community, it sounds, to say the least, a bit disquieting. But the "true aristocracy" is merely the communion of those few individuals who have, each in his unique fashion, realized the possibility of genuine inner existence that is in all men and who reach out to one another in that achievement. What Jaspers is objecting to, as against such rare and hard-won achievement, is the universal predominance of mediocrity as fact and standard in our society. Actually, this same mediocrity, the process of "wearing down into uniformity all that is individual," is more clearly described, from the point of view of the English reader, in Mill's chapter "Of Individuality" in the essay On Liberty. What Jaspers has to say in Die geistige Situation is essentially, despite the differences in terminology, an elaboration of that chapter, as our Hollywood-radio-ridden world is an elaboration of the situation that it describes.

On the other hand, Jaspers' attack on the era of technology is qualified at several points. He recognizes the inevitability of further technical advance and appears to hope that we may yet learn to use such skills in the service, or at least not to the disservice, of the goals of genuine personal existence. And he does not, as Marcel at least appears to do, condemn the methods and attitudes of positive science as such as necessarily destructive of significant human life. He admires Kant too much for that; and more especially his great friendship and reverence for Max Weber made him consider even the extension of scientific techniques to human problems as possible and important. Weber's greatness, he felt, was his ruthless honesty in limiting every sociological investigation to a single section of experience and in refusing to construct a dogmatic philosophy of human life as such out of

[125]

his carefully restricted empirical researches. Such social science is doubly modeled on natural science in the Kantian spirit. It involves the search for truth within a strictly limited area, limited both by the phenomenon studied and by the defining principles applied to it, yet unlimited in the sense that it can never, thanks to its phenomenal nature, be said to be completed. And it leaves, as Kant's science does, an open field for the moral and religious aspirations of men, since in its disciplined objectivity it neither imposes on nor is imposed on by the uniquely inward, outwardly inexpressible conflicts or triumphs of the concrete individual self. Kierkegaard, of course, would find such a separation absurd; but it is an important ingredient in Jaspers' modified existentialism.

A certain respect for positive science is mirrored, too, in Jaspers' treatment of positivism in the first volume of his *Philosophie*.[3] He deals there with positivism and idealism as the two philosophies which have tried, in recent times, to assimilate all reality into a complete and unified system. Both fail, he thinks, when they fail to recognize their own limitations; but they may be useful to genuine, existential philosophizing if they do recognize those limitations. The limit of positivism lies, ultimately, in its inability to know itself and, what is even worse, to live itself: "if I wanted to live positivistically, I should not be myself; this I know more or less consciously and have no rest." The limit of idealism, conversely, lies in its inability to recognize what cannot be understood, the brute facts of empirical reality; or, if it recognizes them, it dismisses them, as Hegel did, as trivial and irrelevant to philosophy. The common use and the common weakness of the two systems lie in their aim of stating unequivocally the whole and completed nature of the real; for in that they at once fulfil a human need and lead to a

3. Karl Jaspers, *Philosophie* (3 vols.; Berlin: Julius Springer, 1932), Vol. I: *Philosophische Weltorientierung*.

danger both of intellectual error and of personal failure. That is not to say that there is no truth in these systems; according to Jaspers, there is no distinction of truth from falsity in philosophy but only the distinction of the honest, genuinely personal search for truth from the arbitrary word-games of system-builders. Therefore, positivism or idealism, in so far as they do spring from genuine philosophizing, may lead "possible existence" to its realization through the very recognition of their systematic limits:

Positivism and idealism are true if they receive their stimulus and limitation from a deeper source. They are not only real but, when they are relativized, true forces in history as we see it and in our own awareness of what exists. Without positivism there is no body, without idealism no space for an objective and meaningful realization of possible existence.[4]

2

To escape the spiritual dangers of our time, then, both these writers turn, in rather different ways, to existential concepts as reminders of those aspects of human nature which should not and cannot be mechanized.

Marcel is careful to specify that in philosophizing in Kierkegaard's tradition he is not denying the validity of the Thomistic Catholic synthesis. But, he says, the irreligious character of our age unhappily renders the great insights of that system valid only for some, not for all, of our contemporaries. So the philosopher must somehow lead bewildered humanity back to the faith by which it used to live and by which it needs to live. And to do this it is necessary to turn to the very concrete problems—or rather, for Marcel, the mysteries deeper than mere problems at the heart of personal existence. Here there is hope of finding the living root from which faith may grow again.

The method which Marcel pursues in this endeavor—if it deserves the name of "method"—is principally that of the

4. *Ibid.*, I, 236.

"metaphysical diary." He published two of these, one under the title *Journal métaphysique* and one forming the major portion of the volume *Être et avoir*. This is, however, not another Cartesian meditation. (In fact, Marcel is as strong in his dislike of all Descartes stands for as Sartre is in his emphasis on the Cartesian cogito as the only valid starting-point for philosophy.) The *Meditations* is the result of a rigorous application of a seriously conceived "scientific" technique of problem-solving. The "Metaphysical Diaries," on the other hand, consist of jottings of day-by-day reflections, sometimes interconnected, sometimes quite random. One finds anything from "Walking with R today, was impressed by what he said about X" to "Today I experienced grace for the first time. . . . . I have never felt such joy." Jean Wahl, in his essay on Marcel in *Vers le concret*,[5] appears to think highly of the *Journal métaphysique* as a philosophical form. True, he is writing of the earlier diary, which seems to have rather more coherence than its sequel in *Être et avoir*; but, all the same, I cannot agree that there is in either of these volumes a philosophic method worthy of serious consideration. The mad dialectic of Kierkegaard makes a good deal more sense than this—not to mention what M. Isère describes as the "brilliantly inaccurate" reasoning of Sartre[6]— inaccurate perhaps, but brilliant certainly in its technique and often even in its insights.

Despite the shortcomings of his method, however, the existential concepts which Marcel stresses are, in part at least, worth noting. Marcel, like Sartre, though with a very different purpose, stresses the importance of body in the analysis of the human individual. But, he feels, one of the great errors of Cartesianism was to substitute body in the abstract for the older and truer Christian conception of the flesh—the flesh that is "the inevitable shortcoming of a fallen creature."

5. Paris: Librairie philosophique J. Vrin, 1932.
6. Jean Isère, "Communication, Sartre vs. Proust?" *Kenyon Review*, IX, No. 2 (spring, 1947), 286–89.

In so far as the human individual lives by and of the flesh, his life centers in possession—in having, first, his body, with its perfections and imperfections, its cravings and fears, and then, through flesh and fleshly desire, the other possessions that dominate his scattered and unceasing dreams and disappointments. And the age of technocracy is, of course, the age of having *in excelsis.*

But there is more to human personality, Marcel thinks, than this "inevitable shortcoming" of our fallen state. There is, beyond the lure of possession, the striving for *being* rather than mere *having.* And this can be satisfied, according to him, only in the "shift of center" of personal existence which constitutes love. Marcel contrasts the "he" ("lui") who is the object of the self-seeking, possessing subject with the "thou," ("toi") revealed by love, who is somehow part of one's self or at one with one's self. This might, if Marcel did anything with it, present a comforting alternative to Sartre's bleak theory of the continuous conflict of myself with *autrui.* But all he does, as far as I can see, is to present, with unctuous sentimentality, a number of generalizing phrases as unconvincing as a very bad sermon on the text "God is love." Take such a passage as this:

How could I confuse this attachment of the soul to its glory, which is only the driest, most strained, most shriveled form of self-love, with what at all times I have called "fidelity"? Is it chance that it is, on the contrary, in those beings least preoccupied with shining in their own eyes that fidelity occurs in its most unexceptionable features? It is a peasant or a servant face that has revealed it to me. And what can be the principle of so ruinous a confusion between two dispositions of the soul, the most superficial judgment of which assures me that they are forever incompatible? How can one help seeing, after all, that a fidelity to another of which I myself was the principle, the root, and the center would, by the clandestine substitution that it conceals, once more establish a lie at the heart of the existence which it informs?[7]

7. Marcel, *op. cit.,* p. 75.

[129]

Nor, to judge, for example, from such a play as *La Chapelle ardente*, is this generalizing backed, in Marcel's literary productions, by such bitter reality as works like *Le Mur* or *L'Age de raison* provide for Sartre's theoretical statements. The substitution of "flesh" (*chair*) for "body" (*corps*) is interesting and perhaps sound, but the theory of "love" and the "thou" as relief from the ills of the flesh has a thoroughly false ring.

That is, I suppose, from Marcel's point of view, only the obtuse reaction of the unbeliever; for the significance of love and the thou lies ultimately in the way in which these concepts subserve the return to faith in God as the center of spiritual life. Faith, Marcel says, is the recognition of God's existence, love of his perfection. But it is faith that gives meaning and possibility to love, for only faith in God makes love and the *thou*—and therewith the approach to being— possible. God is, according to the first "Metaphysical Diary," the "plan of thous," and all love depends on him. Or, as the second diary puts it, the existential project—*l'engagement*— can be meaningful only through God, since it is only through faith that a promise and, therefore, any genuine approach of one self to another can be significant. Without such faith the very idea of a projection of self into the future is meaningless; for the self of desires, of momentary pleasures, of having, cannot depend on itself to feel tomorrow as it does today. Only by God's support is such permanence or, to put it humanly, such loyalty possible. By nature we are all traitors; only divine grace can make us true.

One who does not share Marcel's faith can only comment: this in a way sounds reasonable; but again something about the tone of his writing does not ring true. This is, of course, a very general impression, rather hard to confirm in particulars. One can only quote some passages, for example, one from an essay on "Piety in Peter Wust." Apropos of Cartesian doubt Marcel explains:

A more profound analysis than that of Descartes would permit us to recognize, according to Wust, that at the basis of doubt there is astonishment at one's self.

My doubt betrays the consciousness that I have of my own contingency and—still more implicitly—of the secret gravitation of my most intimate being in relation to an absolute *center* or *middle* of being, not apprehended certainly, but sensed, where the metaphysical insecurity of the creature would finally find its repose. This insecurity, this instability, which contrasts so strangely with the eternal repose or the imperturbable order of nature, constitutes the central mystery of which one can say that the philosophy of Wust is only the deepening. Nowhere today, it seems to me, does one find a more persevering effort to define and to retrieve the metaphysical situation of the human being in relation to an order which it interrupts and transcends, but also to a sovereign Reality which, if it envelops it on all sides, nevertheless never reaches to the relative independence which is its endowment as a creature. For that Reality itself is free and freely sows freedoms.

It is at the core of astonishment, such as we perceive it, for example, in the look of a small child, that there is a rent in the absolute darkness of the natural slumber to which is delivered all that is submitted without restriction to the Law. It is with it that there rises "the sun of the spirit which shines at the horizon of our being . . . . ."

How can one help recognizing here the inspiration which animates the work of our Claudel and which should perhaps guide every authentically Catholic doctrine of knowledge?[8]

One point Marcel does make which seems to me extremely sound and a good deal more honest than many Christian apologists like to be: that is, his emphasis on the primary significance of the concrete experience of faith as essential to so-called "proofs of God." He says, in essence, what Professor Wolfson says in his *Philosophy of Spinoza* about the ontological argument, what in a way Kant said in his refutation of that argument and what even, indirectly, Anselm himself said in his answer to Gaunilon: the absolute, concrete, given fact of faith comes first—"proofs" are only in-

8. *Ibid.*, pp. 321–22.

tellectual elaborations of that faith. They are, at bottom, unnecessary to those who do believe and unconvincing to those who do not. This is, of course, undeniably anti-Thomistic; and I do not know how Marcel would reconcile such a position with his avowed respect for Thomism as a tenable Christian philosophy for those who can grasp its lofty principles. Perhaps, in fact, his concession to Thomism is a particular example of the weakness that one feels in him elsewhere more generally and more vaguely. Aside from the irritating effect of the haphazard diary form, aside even from the repellent sentimentality of much of his writing—though that is near to the central failing of his philosophy—what one feels about the "Metaphysical Diaries" is that, in terms of Jaspers' distinction, this is not genuine philosophizing but a two-faced, ambiguous, and not even very clever imitation of it.

3

If Marcel is using existential concepts to effect a return to the Catholic faith and the church, Jaspers—for whom such a return would be unhistorical and therefore existentially false—is using *Existenzerhellung* to modify and supplement the distinctively Protestant Kantian tradition. Jaspers is not in any technical sense a Kantian, but he is certainly deeply under Kant's influence. That is reflected in the very organization of his *Philosophie*. Its three volumes deal with three essential aspects of human experience: the knowable objective world open to science; the experienced, but unknowable, process of the individual's inner history; and the equally unknowable, yet inexhaustible, symbols of cosmic meaning variously interpreted in art, religion, and metaphysics. The relations between these three spheres appear to be conceived in a manner not unlike the Kantian relation between science, morality, and religion. But the emphasis on the concrete uniqueness of *my* personal existence, of course, involves a radical transformation of the Kantian tradition, with its universal categories and principles in every area. Jaspers indicates at the beginning of the volume on *Existenzerhellung* how, in existential analysis, the Kantian objective categories are transformed:

Objective reality submits to rules and is knowable according to them; existential reality is, without rules, absolutely *historical.* .... The rules of reality are *causal laws;* what happens has cause and effect in temporal succession; existential reality, on the contrary, appears to itself in time from its own origin, i.e., it is *free.* .... Substance is the *permanent in time,* that remains, is neither increased nor diminished; *Existenz* is in the appearance of time vanishing and starting up..... To the *reciprocal causality* of substances .... the *communication* of personal existences is contrasted. Objective reality is whatever corresponds in general to a *sensation;* existential reality is *absoluteness* [*Unbedingtheit*] *in the decisive moment;* to empirical reality corresponds the *content* of the decision..... To time in general .... corresponds this fulfilled time as eternal present. The former is something objective, measurable, and empirically real; the latter is the depth of personal existence out of freedom in its origin. The former is present as valid for everyone; in the latter, time comes into being in choice and decision as appearance at a particular time. *Existenz* has *its* time, not *time as such.* Time as such exists for consciousness in general, the other only for *Existenz* in its historical consciousness..... Objectively *nothing new* can arise as substance. .... Existentially, on the other hand, there is no objectivity .... but there are *leaps and new birth* of *Existenz* in appearance.[9]

The rest of this volume is devoted to the exposition of these "signa" and others like them. Some of the concepts used·are familiar from Kierkegaard—the unconditioned character of the existential resolve as against the conditioned nature of the objectified, sensory world; the individual's history as union of time and eternity; the absoluteness of my freedom and the guilt before God which it entails. The concept of "boundary situation," developed, I believe, from

9. Jaspers, *op. cit.*, II (*Existenzerhellung*), 17–18.

[133]

Jaspers' early medical experience (see his *Psychopathologie*), is a kind of summary of several Kierkegaardian conceptions. All existence is constantly in situation; it must make its choices within the limits of just these particular contingent facts. Yet in such a sheerly given historical situation it must choose *absolutely*. That is again, of course, the conflict of absolute and relative, aspiration and meaningless given, that Kierkegaard and all existentialists after him have stressed. What Jaspers calls "boundary situations" are the crises in human existence in which that conflict and its meaning become most poignantly and tragically clear. He treats four particular ones—death, suffering, struggle, and guilt; and two more general ones—that of the particular historical determination of my particular existence and that of the relativity of all that is real, its self-contradictory character as being always somehow what it is not. In such limiting moments of awareness, existence is shattered by the realization of what it cannot be, but only in these moments does it come to itself as what it genuinely is.

All this is common existential stock-in-trade. What is true in it is said with much greater vigor and precision by either Heidegger or Sartre. As against such common doctrine, the views of Jaspers are distinguished from those of other existentialists principally by his emphasis on *communication* and *transcendence* as the inevitable accompaniments of genuine personal existence. By *communication* he means not, of course, the unreal gregariousness of the social conventions but the direct togetherness of two human beings struggling jointly to realize, always precariously, yet absolutely, the fulfilment of their deepest personal reality. Not only does Jaspers believe that there can be such direct participation of two souls in one another's joys or sorrows; he appears to believe, likewise, that "possible existence" can become reality, that the individual can free himself from the deluding snares of external demands to become, in existential resolve, genuinely himself, *only* in union with another self. Again, as with Marcel, this might constitute a striking rebuttal of Sartre if anything were done with the suggestion. But again, in the case of Jaspers as of Marcel, various theses are suggested about personal existence without either arguments whose logic convinces or concrete examples whose evidence bears them out; so that, much as one might like to, one cannot find in these vague and often unintelligible pronouncements any weapon against the somehow sophistical, yet extremely clever, dialectic of Sartre, or, for that matter, against the desperate loneliness of Kierkegaard or the solitary arrogance of Heidegger. Such a passage as this is typical:

> In communication, through which I know myself touched [*getroffen*], the other is only *this* other: the uniqueness is the appearance of the substantiality of this being. Existential communication is not to be anticipated and not to be imitated but is simply in its momentary single occurrence. It is between two selves, which are only these and not representatives and therefore admit no substitution. The self has its certainty in this communication as absolutely historical, unknowable from without. Only in it is the *self for the self in reciprocal creation*. In historical decision the self has, through binding itself to communication, suspended its selfhood as isolated being-I, in order to grasp selfhood in communication.[10]

The statement is clumsy but not bad, perhaps. Only multiply it several thousand times, and you get a morass of abstractions presumably dealing with the most concrete and vivid of problems, neatly organized under heads and subheads, but carrying no conviction as philosophical argument, no vividness as the expression of an individual life. Knowing the man to be honest and upright in the extreme, I should not say, as I have ventured to guess of Marcel, that the drive back of Jaspers' philosophizing is not genuine. Yet he certainly does lack vitality to carry into any convincing issue whatever it is that he basically wants to convey. Once in a

10. *Ibid.*, p. 58.

[135]

while there is a rather striking epigram, like "wer nur die Menschheit liebt, liebt gar nicht; wohl aber, wer diesen bestimmten Menschen liebt."[11] Sometimes there is a provocative general statement, like the assertion that *Existenz* fulfils itself only where there is some loosing of the bonds between individual and state or society, some break in the naïve identification between them. In general, however, there is a spread-out, swamplike placidity in Jaspers' writing that obscures its truth as well, perhaps, as cloaking its errors. Despite geographical as well as doctrinal differences, I am constantly reminded, when reading him, of Edmund Wilson's description of the atmosphere of Hegelian idealism: ".... The abstractions of the Germans .... are like foggy and amorphous myths, which hang in the gray heavens above the flat land of Königsberg and Berlin, only descending into reality in the role of intervening gods."[12]

All this holds equally of Jaspers' doctrine of *transcendence*. That is, one gathers, the word he uses for God. The conception is broadened, or weakened if you like, to refer to the object of all human gropings for portents and meanings more than merely human, whether personified in a deity, conceptualized in metaphysical systems, or visualized in art. Such a conception has, of course, nothing in common with the *transcendence* of Heidegger and the French school. That transcendence is the projection of the individual into the future, the essence of liberty in a purely human sense. Jaspers' transcendence, though indispensable, in his view, for freedom itself, is by no means identical with it. It is what the individual reaches for as something greater than himself, as an object of worship or at least of wonder. And it is something dimly reached for, never met face to face—not even, like Kierke-

11. *Ibid.*, I, 16: "He does not love at all who loves mankind only; he does who loves this specific person."
12. Edmund Wilson, *To the Finland Station* (New York: Harcourt Brace & Co., 1940), p. 121.

gaard's God, in agony and paradox. All the finite self can do, according to Jaspers, is to read the *Chiffreschrift* of this inexhaustible reality that is forever beyond his direct vision or understanding. In art, religion, and metaphysics one is only reading this puzzling cosmic language in various more or less indirect, but never final, forms.

Such an interpretation of the common function of metaphysical, artistic, and religious activities is probably correct, and should certainly lend itself to illustration with an indefinite range of examples. Yet, once more, we have in Jaspers only a long series of vague and sentimental generalizations, which only dim to the vanishing-point the sense of real, if distorted, religious experience that one feels in someone like Kierkegaard. That Protestantism does mean something very real for Jaspers one knows, for example, from his speech at the opening of the medical faculty in Heidelberg and from the expansion of its theme in *Die Schuldfrage*.[13] But no such living religious tradition shows through the dense mists of the *Philosophie*. When it comes to art, too, though there is nothing especially wrong with his general statements, there are no illuminating particulars to bear them out. In talking of the relation of philosophy to *Existenz*, for instance, he mentions *The Brothers Karamazov*, which is for many obvious reasons a favorite text of existential critics. All Jaspers has to say about it is that it has too much of philosophy for a novel and too much of a novel for philosophy. With all the absurdities of his absurdism, one would vastly prefer the exposition of Camus in his *Mythe de Sisyphe* to that.

One more difficulty: It is not made clear in what way the achievement of freedom by the individual depends on communication with another individual. Nor is it at all appar-

13. Jaspers, *Die Schuldfrage* (Zürich: Artemis Verlag, 1946). This is a powerful and genuinely moving statement of the types of guilt and their atonement, as applied to the present situation of Germany and its people.

ent in what sense the freedom of the individual essentially involves transcendence, or how transcendence is achieved in communication. Jaspers asserts that all these dependencies hold. Without transcendence, he says, one cannot even will. And it seems also that transcendence is discovered only through communication: "No one can save his soul alone." But of reasons for these necessary connections one finds no mention. Granted, of course, that in the sphere of *Existenz* there is no Leibnizian Law of Sufficient Reason nor even Humean necessary connections. Still, the whole purpose of Kierkegaard's indirect communication, of the existential analysis of Heidegger, or of the phenomenology of Sartre is to devise some means, however devious or difficult, of conveying meaningful general truths about this most particular of realities.

4

Looking at both these writers, finally, one feels in them, despite their different aims, a common lack. Marcel would return to the authority of a supreme church to save humanity; Jaspers would go forward stoically with a kind of watered-down Goethean *Stirb' und Werde* as a source of inner salvation amid ruin. Both lack, as existentialists, the terrible realization of dread as the core of human life. Perhaps, indeed, the stress on dread and despair makes existentialism merely another nihilism, a gesture of abnegation rather than a positive philosophy. But it is that stress that gives the movement such significance, however transient, as it obviously does have. When dread turns to good cheer and despair to hope, "existence" becomes merely the catchword for another philosophic system, vaguer and less precise but no more real than most. Marcel finds in Kierkegaard the thinker who saw the *possibility* of dread and its significance for human life. But it is not the possibility of a dread that can be easily obviated by God's good grace that is significant in

Kierkegaard; it is the inescapable *actuality* of dread that, for his twentieth-century successors, forms the living core of his thought. Jaspers, to be sure, acknowledges this actuality: in the boundary situations, or in his final account of *das Scheitern* as, paradoxically, the only fulfilment that our lives can find. Yet his tone is such that one feels, almost smugly, that this sort of failure is a rather comforting sort of success: "Im farb'gen Abglanz haben wir das Leben."

If, moreover, as philosophers, both Marcel and Jaspers lack the force of a precise and vigorous method, that failure follows, in a sense, just because they have disguised the unique function of dread in the existential situation; for it is the reality of dread that impels the logic of the more vigorous existentialists, whether Kierkegaard himself or Heidegger or Sartre. Jean Wahl in the opening issue of *Deucalion* attacks, plausibly enough, many of Sartre's rather forced and tortuous arguments on "nothing" (the object, for him, of dread) in the first hundred papes of *L'Être et le néant*. But then, he asks, why has not Sartre, after disposing of Heidegger's *Sein zum Tode*, got rid of dread itself as so essential to his argument? That would be more comfortable, indeed— but it would not be existentialism, nor would it be anything else of philosophic interest. For every significant philosophy is impelled by some ruling passion, be it even so mild a passion as Hume's love of the gentle and nonviolent or so ascetic a passion as Spinoza's exaltation of reason over passion itself. And that passion, in existentialism, is, in some form or other, what Sartre calls "l'angoisse éthique." Apart from clever sophisms or well-turned phrases, it is the impassioned realization of the utter loneliness and dread of our being-in-the-world, the sense of all that it means to be "condemned to be free," that gives both its logic and its content to existential philosophy. Without such realization, one can achieve, to judge by Marcel and Jaspers, only vague truisms and empty sentimentality. Jean Wahl himself, in fact, a page or two after his question about Sartre and *angoisse*, quotes with eloquent praise the passage on ethical dread (which we also quoted in chap iii): "I emerge alone and in dread in the face of the unique and first project which constitutes my being; all the barriers, all the railings, collapse, annihilated by the consciousness of my liberty. . . . . I decide it, alone, unjustifiable and without excuse." Of such a passage Wahl says: "Let the detractors of Sartre read pages 76 and 77; and they will recognize there, if they have good faith rather than those good intentions that do not lead to Paradise, the philosopher."[14] He is right, I think; and it is the lack of such clear and striking expression of the meaning of dread that is the central weakness of the apparently gentler and more cheering, but infinitely duller, philosophies of Jaspers and Marcel.

14. Jean Wahl, "Essai sur le néant d'un problème," *Deucalion*, I, No. 1 (1946), 39–72.

CHAPTER SEVEN

POSTSCRIPT

And it came to pass after these things, that God did tempt Abra-
ham, and said unto him, Abraham; and he said, Behold, here I am.
And he said, Take now thy son, Isaac, whom thou lovest, and
get thee into the land of Moriah; and offer him there for a burnt
offering upon one of the mountains which I will tell thee of.

. . .

WHAT haunted Kierkegaard in the story of Abraham
and Isaac was the paradox of faith—in particular,
the secret triumph of faith by the very power of
its absurdity against the public ethical demands before which
faith is merely absurd. That Abraham must be silent, that
he cannot communicate God's command, is all-important:
acts expressive of human morality obey general, rational,
communicable principles; but the supreme value, which only
the religious life can claim, lies beyond reason, beyond speech,
in the decisive moment wherein the will submits itself to
God. Morality is the sphere of abstract principles of behavior; to religion alone belongs the unique historical moment, the moment that cannot be told because it tells so
much. For the modern existentialist, though Abraham's faith
may appear as self-delusion, the secrecy, the absurdity, and
the uniqueness of the all-important moment of decision
remain; but they are transferred now to morality itself. There
is no longer any public domain of the ethical—only bad
faith pretends there is—and the temptation of Abraham becomes the symbol not of man before God but of man before
himself. The absurdity, the uniqueness, the inexpressible
significance lie now, as we have seen, in "the tragic ambiguity
of the human situation," which is situation, given, fact-
fettered, and obstinate, yet freely interpreted and even, by

[141]

such interpretation, freely created. It is the secret, puzzling, frightening genesis, against reason and against logic, not of superhuman but of very human values that Kierkegaard's philosophic heirs describe.

The question remains to be asked, though not perhaps to be answered: Once a public morality, an openly given set of moral laws, is denied, *what* values grow out of such secret decisions, and how are they maintained against their own unjustifiability and absurdity? What, if any, morality can be created, a posteriori, out of the two-faced, self-conflicting, forever ambiguous situation of each of us? Kierkegaard's existential dialectic comes to a resting place in faith. It may be, indeed, a resting place as uncomfortable spiritually as a Hindu saint's is physically, for Kierkegaard's life of faith is a life of inner torture, knowing no palliative and no escape. Yet it is, for Kierkegaard, a positive issue of his dialectical progression and a triumph, however agonized, of the human spirit. Is there any issue, any resting place, for the dialectic of the contemporary existentialism? Of course, in one sense there is and can be none, and it is "bad faith" to demand one; for, as existentialists as different as Sartre and Jaspers would agree, philosophy is not system-building but philosophizing. It is thought in action, the very life of the philosopher, which knows no end in the sense of *telos*, only cessation, or continuation in the equally unfinished lives of other actor-thinkers. Yet one can presumably say something about good and evil, even without claiming finality for one's value-system. Certainly, it *is* as an attempt at a new morality that existentialism is chiefly thought of. And, certainly, even aside from the too glibly moralizing "Humanism" essay, one does find in Sartre and his school undeniable indications that it is some sort of new morality, not just a phenomenological description of man's situation (*la condition humaine*), that they are trying to develop. Even in the more austerely intellectual analyses of Heidegger, the distinction between "genuine" and "fraudulent" strongly suggests (especially if one is acquainted with the platform personality of the author) a depreciation of the latter in favor of the former. In fact, one can say of contemporary existentialism in general that the distinction between everyday self-delusion and the profounder awareness of one's freedom achieved in the rare and rarely revealing moment implies, however it be presented, an evaluative preference intelligible only in the light of a self-conscious and statable moral standard.

If one looks for such a standard in existentialism, then, the first thing one finds is, as we have seen, that freedom itself, for Sartre and Heidegger at any rate, appears as the source of ultimate value. Values are generated by our free decisions: they start up, Sartre declares, like partridges before our acts. Yet the *only* value, it seems, that can stand against the charge of bad faith, the only self-justifying value, is the value of that very free decision itself. Acts done and lives lived in bad faith are those in which we cloak from ourselves the nature of our freedom, in which, to escape dread, we try to make our subjectivity into an object and so, though, of course, we do act freely even in such self-deception, we betray our freedom by disguising it.

To be sure, one may say that, in such a situation, the ultimate value is honesty rather than freedom. We are free in any case; from that fact, both glorious and fearful, there is no escape as long as we live at all. But it is a fact that we may or may not face honestly. Good for the individual resides in the integrity with which he recognizes his freedom and acts while so recognizing it. Evil, conversely, is the lie of fraudulent objectivity, the denial of freedom. In this sense, for example, it is consistent in Sartre, though startling in the context of his extremely factual description, to call masochism a "vice," since masochism is the endeavor to make myself completely and abjectly a mere thing before my own consciousness as well as before another's; and so it is the extremest self-deception, the completest possible rejection of my liberty. And it is apt enough, more generally, to say that existentialism is an ethic of *integrity*, in which running away from one's self is evil, facing one's self is good.

But integrity is not a mere intellectual quality. It is not solely a question, for the existentialist, of being honest in *seeing* one's freedom and its nature. It is integrity of character and action rather than of vision alone that is to be prized. True, there is no *choice* between acting freely and nonfreely. That is the only choice that we do *not* have. We must be free, even in the vain attempt to relinquish freedom. But there *is* a choice between acting in the full awareness of freedom and acting in the endeavor to escape it; and such a choice implies not only the difference between honesty and dishonesty but a difference in the ends of action as well. Action in the full light of freedom, it is clear in both Sartre and Heidegger, is not only honest action but action *for the sake of freedom:* that end, not the honesty involved in seeking it, is the ultimate self-justifying good. And the fraudulence of bad faith, on the other side, lies as much in the counterfeit character of the values sought as in the dishonesty of the attempt to seek them. There is serious meaning in the joke about Heidegger's student, who declared in all solemnity: "I am resolved—only I don't know to what!" ("Ich bin entschlossen—ich weiss nur nicht wozu"); for it is the structure of the free resolve *in* its freedom, not any value beyond it, for the sake of which, in Heidegger's view, the free man acts. And for Sartre, too, in his personal as well as his political philosophy it is freedom itself, in all its tormenting uncertainty, and freedom only, that the honest man must seek. Mathieu, despite—or, better, because of—the negativity of his actions, is the proper carrier of Sartre's ethical philosophy; for, in all his decisions, whatever positive value is presented as a lure to action collapses in the light of its possible fraudulence and only freedom itself stands, on the other side, as the single and difficult good for which all else must be denied.

Perhaps in the outcome of the *Paths of Freedom*, in the third volume of Sartre's trilogy, Mathieu's and Sartre's morality may emerge with some new synthesis, some other content sought for than sheer liberty for the sake of itself. Yet in the light of present evidence, one cannot help doubting the likelihood of such an issue and wondering, meanwhile, how freedom as the sole and self-sufficient moral standard can operate. Existentialism provides, as we have seen, no adequate means of elevating the individual's search for freedom to the status of a universal principle. It is not man as free being, in general, that existential philosophy can ask us to respect. It can demand only that each of us, solitary and unbefriended, seek his own freedom. Such a demand is, in fact, it seems to me, a legitimate moral claim. Therein lies the genuine strength of the philosophy that expresses it, with its telling revelations, on the social as well as the individual level, of the infinite varieties of bad faith by which most of us allow ourselves to pretend to live. On the other hand, to place the *sole* good in freedom seems, when one looks closer, to invalidate the very description of the free act itself that existential philosophy has given. Take Sartre's analysis of taste, quoted above: even the most trivial taste, he says, is not capricious but is an expression of the fundamental project that is the man himself; that is clear from the fact that it presents itself as an evident value—we are always astonished when others fail to apprehend it as we do. Such a description implies, it seems to me, an indefinite plurality of values, almost a "realm of values" in which we *find* our goods and evils, not a starting-up of formerly nonexistent partridges before our acts. Or take the examples that we mentioned earlier of typically "existential" situations. Sartre's Garcin, we said, has to face forever the hell of interpreting his own action, which was cowardly. Conrad's Lord Jim must pass through the purgatory of atonement for his act, which was dishonorable. But a man can be cowardly or dishonorable only if he *already* believes in the value of courage or honor.

[145]

Those values are not created by his acts but are already implicit in the acts. Even supposing that I have made the wrong judgment in these particular cases, suppose Garcin was not a coward or Lord Jim in fact a man dishonored; the moral situation remains the same, the standard of courage or honor is found in, not made by, the situation. True, Sartre admits that we are always already *engaged* in projects, involved in the values which we have chosen—hence, he might say, the a priori *look* of values in such cases. But they are still values that we have chosen and, in that sense, have made for ourselves out of what, without our agency, would be a meaningless, valueless succession of mere facts. Yet that is not, I think, a sufficient answer. It is quite true that we have, in the deepest sense, chosen our own values; and the description of that choice, in its absurd and dreadful finality, is the existentialist's undeniable merit. But we have chosen them, in the existentialist's own terms, in situation. We have not made them out of whole cloth but have chosen them out of a series of alternatives offered us—offered us by personal disposition, national tradition, the chance influence of other personalities, and so on. Again, the existentialist would probably answer that he certainly does take into account the limits of situation. Facticity as well as freedom, freedom-in-facticity, is what he is trying to describe. But somehow—as is apparent, for instance, in the treatment of history in Sartre[1] as well as in Heidegger—the backward stress is not so effective in the final issue as is the forward one. So Sartre can ask: *What, then, is a value if not the call of that which is not yet?*

But a value is also the appeal of what has been; and perhaps one can say, very tentatively, that what the existentialists lack is a conception of something like tradition or community

1. The explicit treatment of history in *L'Être et le néant* is admittedly brief, but it does seem rather forced and narrow in comparison with other aspects of Sartre's analysis.

on which to ground their view of freedom. In our libertarian tradition the demand for the universal sanctity of human freedom is probably identical with the conception of community. In that case it is, for the account of our own situation, the inability of the existentialists to expand and generalize their stress on the freedom of the individual that is at fault. But, for man in general, as distinct from modern European man, there is not necessarily any such identity; and if existentialism is in any sense what it claims to be—an analysis of man, not merely a Western twentieth-century self-portrait—its limitation appears in the defect of the broader concept.

I do not mean to suggest, however, that existentialism may develop a concept of community or historical tradition to counterbalance the narrowness of its peculiar individualism and thereby conveniently furnish, as an additional dimension in its analysis of man, a broader basis for morality to supplement the depth of its limited insights. Such easy polarity of balancing one factor against another would only dull the edge of those insights, would substitute a Jaspers or Marcel, for instance, for a Sartre or Heidegger. Genuine philosophic syntheses are not so easily achieved.

That the difficulty lies deeper than that, in the very nature of value theory itself, is evident, for example, if one compares the existential morality with Kant's. For Kant, as for the existentialists, freedom, not any substantive good, is the central moral concept. Moreover, for Kant, as for the existentialists, freedom is curiously inwrought with its opposite, the subjective pole of our responsible, nonsensuous being with our objective existence as parts of nature. Kant's "sensuous" and "supersensuous" are worlds apart, yet necessarily coexistent; and it is out of that essential conjunction of essential opposites that morality springs. But for Kant it is the opposition of two abstractions. Duty and inclination are every man's, not mine. And proportionate to their abstractness is the ease with which the one is held subordinate to the other by the inevitable rightness of the moral law. The usual claim of overabstractness against the categorical imperative is often made on superficial grounds—because, for instance, for the supporters of an "empirical" morality, whatever is a priori is, *ipso facto*, wrong. But there is truth back of the objection, all the same. In the theoretical sphere Kant was genuinely puzzled, and out of his puzzlement grew a critique of knowledge that was truly the great event of modern philosophy. But in the field of practical reason he had no doubts. He was happily at home in an unquestioned moral-religious tradition; and in that situation a solution came easily because there was, at bottom, no problem to be solved. True, the practical imperative: Treat every person as an end and never as a means, is again, I should agree, the great modern statement of the basic law which an adequate morality *ought* to state. But to the imposing rightness of such a general statement one must contrast the human wrongness of much of Kant's particular reasoning—the hideous unloveliness of his misanthrope-philanthropist; the absurdity of his direct application of the Law of Contradiction, in its bare abstractness, as a test for moral conduct; and so on. There is a grand moral vista here that is right; but it is achieved at the sacrifice of a more concretely human vision, that of the stumbling, uncertain, half-blind, half too-far-seeing process by which alone, in each single living person, moral values can arise. So one gets a system of value not as solution to, but as substitute for, the *problem* of value. In the existentialists, on the other hand, the *problem* of values, the dilemma that is our human destiny, is envisaged in philosophic argument and in literary or journalistic portraiture in all the terrible reality of its concrete, factual existence. To say that in that picture a general principle like the Kantian is lacking is not to ask for its superimposition but to admit the radical opposition of the two kinds of analysis, despite their superficial likeness;

[148]

for there is, once again, no place in Sartre or Heidegger (or Kierkegaard, for that matter) for such a general morality to take hold. The existentialists' account of the human situation, their concrete apprehension of the nature of the value-problem, its nature as a living, inescapable reality for each individual person, illuminates at many points the dilemma of ourselves and our time, perhaps even of humanity. But its very concreteness, the very brilliance of its insights, preclude a general solution. And the Kantian solution, on the other hand, is a solution because it does *not* see the problem, because it rests on a quiet assurance of its own universality and objectivity, which is, existentially speaking, in this as in every other completed and systematic morality, the product of bad faith. Existentialism, in other words, does not take us in the last analysis beyond the position of the early Nietzsche, where we are faced, ethically, with the choice of honest despair or self-deceiving hope. We can lie to ourselves for the sake of knowing what is good, or face, bravely but drearily, the insufficiency of such "objective" goods. We can face the problem of value, or solve it, never having faced it. But we cannot put the question *and* answer it, see the dilemma *and* escape it. And even that alternative is a Hobson's choice. Once we have faced our freedom and have seen the absurd necessity of our claim to be more than things, once we have granted that "man is unjustifiable," we cannot consciously and willingly turn to self-deception for our escape. Existentialism is a courageous and an honest attempt at a new morality. It may yet be one. But, to the present writer at least, it seems more likely that this is not the new morality we may hope for, but only a new, subtler, and more penetrating statement of our old disheartenment, a new expression of an old despair.

[149]

BIBLIOGRAPHICAL NOTE

KIERKEGAARD

The principal writings of Søren Kierkegaard have been made available in English, chiefly by the Princeton University Press. Of the accounts of his life and work the following may be mentioned:

GEISMAR, E. O. *Lectures on the Religious Thought of S. Kierkegaard*. Minneapolis, Minn.: Augsburg Pub. House, 1937.

LOWRIE, WALTER. *Kierkegaard*. New York: Oxford University Press, 1938.

———. *A Short Life of Kierkegaard*. Princeton: Princeton University Press, 1942.

SWENSON, DAVID. *Something about Kierkegaard*. Minneapolis, Minn.: Augsburg Pub. House, 1941.

HEIDEGGER AND SARTRE

Some of the novels, plays, and essays of Sartre have been appearing in English. To date the following are available:

"The Flies" and "In Camera." London: H. Hamilton, 1946.

The Age of Reason. ("Paths of Freedom," Vol. I.) New York: Alfred A. Knopf, 1947.

The Reprieve. ("Paths of Freedom," Vol. II.) New York: Alfred A. Knopf, 1947.

Existentialism. Translation of the essay *L'Existentialisme est-il un humanisme?* New York: Philosophical Library, 1947.

Portrait of the Anti-Semite. "Partisan Review Pamphlets," No. 1.

For discussions of contemporary existentialism see

BARRETT, WILLIAM. *What Is Existentialism?* "Partisan Review Pamphlets," No. 2.

BROCK, WERNER. *An Introduction to Contemporary German Philosophy.* Cambridge: Cambridge University Press, 1947.

RUGGIERO, GUIDO DE. *Existentialism.* London: Secker & Warburg, 1946.

JASPERS AND MARCEL

The only English title I know of here is the very unsatisfactory translation of *Die geistige Situation der Gegenwart:*

Man in the Modern Age. New York: Henry Holt & Co., 1933.